Culture and
Customs of Mozambique

Mozambique. Cartography by Bookcomp, Inc.

Culture and Customs
of Mozambique

∽o∾

GEORGE O. NDEGE

Culture and Customs of Africa
Toyin Falola, Series Editor

GREENWOOD PRESS
Westport, Connecticut • London

Library of Congress Cataloging-in-Publication Data

Ndege, George O.
　Culture and customs of Mozambique / George O. Ndege.
　　　p. cm.　(Culture and customs of africa, ISSN 1530–8367)
　Includes bibliographical references and index.
　ISBN 0–313–33163–4 (alk. paper)
　1. Ethnology—Mozambique.　2. Mozambique—Social life and customs.
I. Title.
　GN659.M6N34　2007
　306.09679—dc22　　　2006025373

British Library Cataloguing in Publication Data is available.

Library of Congress Catalog Card Number: 2006025373
ISBN-10:　0–313–33163–4
ISBN-13:　978–0–313–33163–3
ISSN:　　1530–8367

First published in 2007

Greenwood Press, 88 Post Road West, Westport, CT 06881
An imprint of Greenwood Publishing Group, Inc.
www.greenwood.com

Printed in the United States of America

The paper used in this book complies with the
Permanent Paper Standard issued by the National
Information Standards Organization (Z39.48–1984).

10　9　8　7　6　5　4　3　2　1

Contents

Series Foreword

AFRICA IS A VAST continent, the second largest, after Asia. It is four times the size of the United States, excluding Alaska. It is the cradle of human civilization. A diverse continent, Africa has more than fifty countries with a population of over 700 million people who speak over 1,000 languages. Ecological and cultural differences vary from one region to another. As an old continent, Africa is one of the richest in culture and customs, and its contributions to world civilization are impressive indeed.

Africans regard culture as essential to their lives and future development. Culture embodies their philosophy, worldview, behavior patterns, arts, and institutions. The books in this series intend to capture the comprehensiveness of African culture and customs, dwelling on such important aspects as religion, worldview, literature, media, art, housing, architecture, cuisine, traditional dress, gender, marriage, family, lifestyles, social customs, music, and dance.

The uses and definitions of "culture" vary, reflecting its prestigious association with civilization and social status, its restriction to attitude and behavior, its globalization, and the debates surrounding issues of tradition, modernity, and postmodernity. The participating authors have chosen a comprehensive meaning of culture while not ignoring the alternative uses of the term.

Each volume in the series focuses on a single country, and the format is uniform. The first chapter presents a historical overview in addition to information on geography, economy, and politics. Each volume then proceeds to examine the various aspects of culture and customs. The series highlights the mechanisms for the transmission of tradition and culture across generations: the significance of orality, traditions, kinship rites, and family property distribution; the rise of print culture; and the impact of educational institutions. The series also explores the intersections between local, regional, national, and global bases for identity and social relations. While the volumes are organized nationally, they pay attention to ethnicity and language groups and the links between Africa and the wider world.

The books in the series capture the elements of continuity and change in culture and customs. Custom is represented not as static or as a museum artifact but as a dynamic phenomenon. Furthermore, the authors recognize the current challenges to traditional wisdom, which include gender relations, the negotiation of local identities in relation to the state, the significance of struggles for power at national and local levels and their impact on cultural traditions and community-based forms of authority, and the tensions between agrarian and industrial/manufacturing/oil-based economic modes of production.

Africa is a continent of great changes, instigated mainly by Africans but also through influences from other continents. The rise of youth culture, the penetration of the global media, and the challenges to generational stability are some of the components of modern change explored in the series. The ways in which traditional (non-Western and nonimitative) African cultural forms continue to survive and thrive—that is, how they have taken advantage of the market system to enhance their influence and reproductions—also receive attention.

Through the books in this series, readers can see their own cultures in a different perspective, understand the habits of Africans, and educate themselves about the customs and cultures of other countries and people. The hope is that the readers will come to respect the cultures of others and see them not as inferior or superior to theirs but merely as different. Africa has always been important to Europe and the United States, essentially as a source of labor, raw materials, and markets. Blacks are in Europe and the Americas as part of the African diaspora, a migration that took place primarily because of the slave trade. Recent African migrants increasingly swell their number and visibility. It is important to understand the history of the diaspora and the newer migrants as well as the roots of the culture and customs of the places from where they come. It is equally important to understand others in order to be able to interact successfully in a world that keeps shrinking. The accessible nature of the books in this series will contribute to this understanding and enhance the quality of human interaction in a new millennium.

Toyin Falola
Frances Higginbothom, Nalle Centennial Professor in History
The University of Texas at Austin

Preface

THIS BOOK IS about the traditions and customs of Mozambique. It proceeds on the premise that tradition and culture are dynamic and dialectical, internal and external processes that shape the worldview of people at a given point in time. The book highlights the rich Mozambican cultural diversity by examining the interplay of many and varied factors ranging from religion and the arts to politics and the family. The factors are examined against the backdrop of the country's historical development and cultural heritage. In this regard, there are two important observations about the use of the terms traditional and modern as well as the general scope of this book.

First, the use of the word traditional or indigenous is for informational purposes and to draw a distinction between a lifestyle that defined most Mozambican societies in the recent past and one that is increasingly being embraced by those who have acquired modern education, live in the urban areas, and participate in the mainstream economy. Modern and contemporary are about the emerging present. Yet, the dialogue between the traditional and the modern revealed in this book shows a society that is experiencing great change and whose indigenous institutions and ways of life are being heavily impacted by forces that define the emerging present.

Second, Mozambique is ethnically diverse. Each ethnic group has certain unique attributes that define and characterize the evolution and development of its institutions as well as its way of life. The ethnic groups have a shared relationship built through history, social and economic interactions, and coexistence in the given geographical space of Mozambique. The contribution of various communities to the making of the comprehensiveness of Mozambican culture is quite evident. This book strives to focus on the common Mozambican culture by highlighting how religion, worldview, arts, literature, education, and colonialism as well as postcolonial experience have collectively contributed to the making of contemporary society.

As people's perceptual preferences and socioeconomic orientation shift to embrace modern values, it is hoped that this book will help facilitate dialogue between the past and emerging present in Mozambique. It should also help readers understand the continuous process of change that has defined and continues to shape contemporary Mozambican society.

Acknowledgments

ALTHOUGH I ALONE am responsible for any errors, distortions, and intellectual weaknesses this book demonstrates, my debts to others who made this project possible are enormous.

The original suggestion that I write a book on the culture and customs of Mozambique came from the series editor, Toyin Falola, one of the leading Africanists of our time, to whom I am much indebted. The footnotes reveal some of my debts to other authors, especially writers on various aspects of Mozambican society, past and present.

The Greenwood editorial team of Wendi Schnaufer, Linda Ellis-Stiewing, Kaitlin Ciarmello, and Tiffany Seisser has been a congenial group with which to work. I received gracious support from Saint Louis University through the SLU 2000 initiative in support of my work during the writing of this book.

Carol Kreamer, Director of the United Methodist Church Missouri Province, sponsored Mozambique Initiative, and Dan and Robin Been of the Baptist Church proved to be some of the most supportive friends by supplying most of the photographs used in this book. Their assistance is not only acknowledged, but also appreciated.

Chronology

3rd century	Iron Age Bantu-speaking communities move into area from west-central Africa.
11th century	Shona empire develops in the area between the Limpopo and Zambezi rivers.
12th–15th centuries	Arab traders dominate the coastal trade between the Mozambican coast and Arabia.
1498	Portuguese navigator Vasco da Gama arrives.
1498–1752	Mozambique administered by governor general of Goa (India).
16th–17th centuries	Portuguese venture into interior. Colonists set up trading posts and mining ventures.
18th–19th centuries	Mozambique becomes major slave-trading center.
1820s	Soshangane, a Nguni warlord from the Northern Nguni in what is today South Africa, invades southern Mozambique and founds the Gaza kingdom.
1842	Portugal outlaws slave trade from Mozambique. However, clandestine trade continues for decades.
1878	Portugal leases large tracts of territory to trading companies.
1891	Portugal and Britain define Mozambique's western and southern borders.
1895–1917	Portuguese pacification wars.
1902	Lourenco Marques (present day Maputo) becomes colonial capital.

1917	The Barue revolt, coordinated by spirit mediums, against Portuguese colonial rule.
1932	Portugal breaks up trading companies and imposes direct rule over the colony.
1950s–1960s	Colonial economy thrives. New Portuguese settlers arrive, especially after World War II.
1962	The Mozambique Liberation Front (Frelimo) is founded under the leadership of Eduardo Mondlane.
1963	Frelimo's first batch of 250 recruits goes to Algeria for military training.
1964	Frelimo forces begin war of independence.
1969	Eduardo Mondlane, Frelimo's leader, is assassinated. Samora Machel replaces him.
1974	Military coup in Lisbon puts power in the hands of National Salvation headed by General Antonio de Spinola. The new government supports autonomy for colonies. Portugal and Frelimo sign an accord in Lusaka, Zambia, which establishes transitional government.
1975	Mozambique attains independence under the leadership of Samora Machel. Many Portuguese settlers leave Mozambique.
1976	Anti-Frelimo resistance group, Renamo, is established by Mozambican rebels, apartheid South Africa, and the South Rhodesian regime.
1977	Under the leadership of Samora Machel, Frelimo adopts Marxist-Leninist doctrine. Frelimo becomes the sole political party and becomes synonymous with the state.
1984	President Samora Machel and P. W. Botha, prime minister of South Africa, sign the Nkomati Accord.
1986	President Samora Machel is killed in a mysterious airplane crash. Joachin Chissano succeeds him as president.
1989	Frelimo formally abandons its commitment to the Marxist-Leninist ideology. Mozambique embraces political and economic reforms.
1990	A new constitution that allows for multiparty elections and a free market economy is promulgated.
1992	A U.S.–negotiated peace accord between Mozambican government and Renamo rebel forces is signed.
1994	National elections are held in December and President Chissano and the ruling Frelimo party emerge victorious.

1995   Mozambique becomes Commonwealth member. The government also publishes its Strategy for Poverty Reduction in Mozambique program, which sets out for the first time explicit policies for poverty reduction in the country.

1999   Chissano defeats Renamo's Dhaklama in presidential elections. The boards of International Development Association and the Fund agree to a set of significant enhancements to the HIPC (Heavily Indebted Poor Country) Initiative in order to reduce the debt burden on Mozambique.

2000   Heavy rains, the highest recorded in 100 years, hit Mozambique. The devastating floods kill 700 people and displace nearly 500,000.

2004   General Elections. Frelimo emerges victorious with 62 percent of the vote.

2005   Armando Guebuza is sworn in as president to replace Joachin Chissano.

1

Introduction

THE REPUBLIC OF MOZAMBIQUE IS located in the southeastern part of Africa. It lies along the Indian Ocean and is bordered by South Africa and Swaziland to the southwest, Zimbabwe to the west, Malawi and Zambia to the north-west, and Tanzania to the north. Mozambique occupies a strategic location because it is the gateway to the hinterland countries of Malawi, Zambia, Zimbabwe, Botswana, and Swaziland. The country is almost a third as wide as it is long at its broadest point. Its longest distance from east to west is 380 miles, while it is 1,120 miles long from north to south. Its coastline is 1,737 miles. The country covers a total area of 309,500 square miles. It is about twice the size of the state of California.

Mozambique has an estimated population of nineteen million people.[1] Slightly more than half, 52 percent, are women. The population is predominantly African. The other groups are Europeans, Euro-Africans, and Indians. These constitute less than 1 percent of the population. The population is generally young, with 43 percent below the age of 14 and just 3 percent above the age of 65.[2] The birth rate is 35.79 per 1,000 of population, while the death rate is 20.99 deaths per 1,000.[3] Infant mortality rates average 130.79 deaths per 1,000 live births.[4] Life expectancy at birth averages 40.32 years.[5] Lower life expectancy, higher infant mortality, and death rates are some of the major challenges that confront the government in its efforts to stabilize population growth and development. A majority of the population lives in rural areas and derives its livelihood from agriculture. The rural/urban ratio is 65/35.[6] Over two-thirds of the population live below the poverty line of approximately U.S.$0.41 per day, with 81 percent residing in the rural areas. More people are migrating to the cities, and it is expected that by 2015 more than 51 percent of the population will live in urban areas.

The capital of Mozambique is Maputo, which is in the south. It is the preeminent center of finance, industry, and trade. The second largest city is Beira, which is a seaport. Most of the major cities are located on the east coast. Since attaining independence from Portugal in 1975, Mozambique has gone through two major phases in its historical development.[7] The period between 1977 and 1991 constitutes the first phase, which was characterized by attempts to build a socialist society based on Marxist-Leninist principles.[8] During this phase civil war raged and led to the deaths of thousands, the displacement of many more, and destruction of the infrastructure. The second phase, from 1992 to the present, has seen the evolution and development of a more market-oriented economy, an open political system, and a return to peace after several decades of war.[9] The major highlights of this latter period include the introduction of a new constitution, rehabilitation of the infrastructure, and a focus on the development of health as well as educational services.

LAND

Mozambique is a moderate plateau. Nearly half the country is 200 meters above sea level. The altitude decreases from the hinterland to the Indian Ocean. Thus the Mozambican coastline is low lying and consists of either swamps or sandy beaches. Mount Binga, located in the mountainous region in the western part of the country bordering Zimbabwe, is the highest peak and measures about 8,200 feet above sea level. The Great Rift Valley also traverses the southern part of the country.

The country is endowed with many rivers, the most important of which is the Zambezi, which divides Mozambique into two roughly equal parts, its northern and southern halves. Cabora Bassa, which is one of the largest hydroelectric projects in Africa, is built on the Zambezi River. The Zambezi is a vital natural resource in the economy of Mozambique. The other major rivers include Ruvuma in the north and Limpopo in the south. Mozambique has a total of 25 rivers. The drainage system is vital in the development of agriculture because it provides fertile soil for the farming activities. Agriculture is the backbone of the Mozambican economy—most Mozambicans derive their livelihood from agriculture.

The climate in Mozambique varies from subtropical to tropical. The southern parts of the country experience a subtropical climate, which gives way to a tropical climate as one moves north. The climate is also influenced by a number of factors such as geography, altitude, and the drainage system.

The northern part of the country experiences high temperatures because of its tropical monsoon climate. In contrast, the southern part is in the subtropical anticyclonic zone. It is drier than the north and its rainfall is low and sporadic. Mozambique has two main seasons: wet and dry. The rainy season begins in October and ends in March. More rain falls in the months of November to March. The dry spell is from April to September. Rainfall during the wet season averages 32 inches, and the temperature averages 30 degrees. Drought is common in the south. The interior highlands are generally cooler than the coastal parts. Rainfall decreases as one descends to the coastal plain.

The vegetation patterns are determined mainly by climate. The coastal part is characterized by sand dunes and beaches as well as swamps, especially where the rivers empty their waters into the Indian Ocean. In the immediate hinterland is the grassland terrain. Forests are found along the river valleys. The central plateau is characterized by extensive grassland. Tropical forests are found in the western highland areas. The vegetation is critical in explaining the economic patterns in the country. Crops such as sugar cane and rice are grown mainly in the river valleys. Tea and tobacco are grown in the highland areas, where timber is also found in plenty. Sisal, cashew nuts, and coconuts are grown in the coastal plain. The extensive grassland is the home to the wildlife that fosters tourism.

Altitude, vegetation, good climate, and rich soils have combined to contribute to the development of agriculture as the most vibrant sector of the economy and the sector from which most of the population derives its livelihood. These features have not, however, always worked to the advantage of the Mozambicans. Heavy rains and subsequent floods have often brought devastation to the people of Mozambique, resulting in the deaths of hundreds, displacement of thousands, and destruction of crops.

PEOPLES

Mozambique, like most African countries, is a multiethnic society. It comprises 16 ethnic groups, most of which are of Bantu origin. Each group speaks its own language, although it is not uncommon for clans within each group to speak different dialects of the same language. Shared language, history, lineage, and cultural practices and customs are what define an ethnic community. Most ethnic groups in Mozambique migrated into their present homeland from other parts of southern Africa. They are related to their kinsmen in the present day South Africa, Swaziland, Zimbabwe, Malawi, and Tanzania. In the course of their migration and settlement in Mozambique, these ethnic groups absorbed disparate and small communities as well as their diverse cultural customs and practices.

The Zambezi valley, which has for centuries been a meeting place of many different societies, is important in understanding the nature and pattern of the settlement of various ethnic communities in modern-day Mozambique. Societies who inhabit the region north of the Zambezi valley speak languages that are akin to their neighbors in Malawi, Zambia, and Tanzania. Those who occupy the region south of the valley, especially in the extreme south, are closely related to the communities in South Africa, Swaziland, and Zimbabwe. The northeastern part of the country adjacent to the coastline is peopled by communities whose political, economic, and cultural organization has been influenced by external groups such as the Arabs. The ethnic groups in Mozambique have not been immune from cultural influences, both from within and outside southern Africa.

The largest ethnic group is the Makua, who live in the north-central part of the country. The Makonde, who are famous for their carvings, inhabit the northern part of the country south of the Ruvuma River bordering Tanzania. They practice agriculture as well as fishing. The Swahili, most of whom are Muslims, live in the northeastern coast. The Swahili embraced Islam as a result of their interaction with Arab traders. The Swahili built city-states along the East African coast long before the advent of Portuguese rule in the late fifteenth century.[10] Sofala is one such city-state. The trade reached its peak during the fourteenth century. Dyed textiles were produced at Sofala and exchanged for gold from the interior.

The extreme southern part of the country is inhabited by the Tonga, which is the second largest ethnic group. The Tonga are an offshoot of the Zulu, and they have inhabited the region bordering South Africa since the nineteenth century. The Nguni live in the south around Maputo. The Nguni practice agriculture and raise livestock as well. They are closely related to the Zulu and the Khoisan groups of southern Africa. The migration of the Zulu- and Nguni-related communities is mainly the result of the upheavals that characterized southern Africa in the nineteenth century during the Mfecane wars.[11] It is not surprising that most of the communities in the extreme south of Mozambique share cultural practices and customs with their Bantu groups in the neighboring states to the south and west. The Chicunda, Maravi, Shona, and Tawara inhabit the central part of Mozambique.

LANGUAGE

The official language of Mozambique is Portuguese. It is the language of commerce, law, and government. English is also encouraged to promote interactions with the neighboring countries, all of which were former British colonies where English is widely used as the official language. English is taught in secondary schools. Mozambique is a member of regional organizations such as SADC and COMESA as well as international organizations such as the Commonwealth, which are dominated by countries that have English as the official language. English is occasionally used in Maputo in transacting business with those from English-speaking countries. With globalization and integration of the economies in the southern Africa region, English is likely to gain prominence in Mozambique.

Portuguese is associated with the formal educational system and is spoken primarily by those who have been formally educated. English is also associated with formal education. Most of the population speaks their mother tongues. As already mentioned, there are many local languages, since every ethnic community has its own language. For example, the Makua speak Emakhuwa, the Tonga Xitsonga, the Makonde Shimaconde, the Swahili Kiswahili, and the Yao Ciyao. Local dialects are not uncommon in a language. Because most of the communities are of Bantu origin these various languages have some general similarities because of shared Bantu root words. There appears to be an established set of attitudes that allows members of the various subethnic groups to perceive themselves as belonging to a single linguistic and cultural community. The Frelimo attempts to do away with Portuguese as the official language after independence were unsuccessful. There was no single dominant African language that had a wide national appeal acceptable to all the communities.

Kiswahili is the most widely spoken local language in the northeastern part of the country and along the coast. As already noted, the Swahili and Islamic influence along the Mozambican coast predates the advent of Portuguese rule in Eastern Africa. Arab traders and Swahili communities were influential along the East African coast for several centuries before the arrival of the Portuguese. During the peak of Arab and Swahili political and economic power, Kiswahili and Arabic were the two preeminent languages of commerce and government. Kiswahili continues to be widely spoken in the northeastern part of the country because of the influence from Tanzania in the north, where it remains popular and is both the national and official language alongside English.

EDUCATION

The modern educational system is one of the most important means of realizing political and economic development. In the context of Mozambique, and indeed in most of the developing countries, it provides teenagers from humble origins with the opportunity to make their way into the middle- and upper-income levels. The development and growth of Western formal education in Mozambique was rather slow. The Portuguese colonial administration paid insignificant attention to education. The aim was to produce a small group of literate Africans who would serve the colonial administration as clerks, court interpreters, and, in the case of the Christian missions, catechists. Some of these indigenous Africans were co-opted into the Portuguese colonial system by being given civil rights in appreciation of their elite status as well as service to the colonial state. As *assimilados,* they were esteemed. In contrast, the *indigenas,* those who were not classified as assimilados, were often subjected to brutal oppression and discrimination.

The Portuguese colonial curriculum was wanting. The content was more focused on European history and culture. The African history, culture, and values were given insufficient attention. Access to education was fairly limited.[12] Few of those who completed primary education proceeded to secondary school because postsecondary education remained largely undeveloped. The Portuguese attempts at expanding educational opportunities during the last decade of colonial rule were not successful because of the war of liberation. The war disrupted learning in the rural areas because of insecurity.

The Frelimo government made concerted efforts to expand educational opportunities for its citizenry after it assumed power in 1975. The government nationalized education by taking over mission schools and removing religion from the curriculum.[13] This drastic action was in line with the regime's Marxist orientation. By 2003, 48 percent of the population was literate, down from a 90 percent illiteracy rate at independence in 1975. The government prioritized education with the goal of eradicating illiteracy. The provision of basic education became an integral part of the national agenda because of its significance as a requisite for social and economic development. The government efforts have so far yielded positive results, especially after the end of the civil war. Between 1994 and 1998 the gross primary school admission rate increased from 58 to 79 percent.[14] By 1999–2000 an estimated 85 percent of primary-school-aged children attended school. Despite these efforts there still exists gender imbalance, because more boys than girls attend school. As a result, the percentage of illiterate girls is higher than that of illiterate boys. Disparity also exists between urban and rural settings. Rural schools are few for the number of school-age children in those areas.

Students are tested at the end of seven years of primary education. Successful candidates proceed to secondary schools. Competition for the few available places in secondary schools is usually stiff, with only a few being selected to proceed with high-school education. In 1999–2000 only 14 percent of secondary-school-aged children were enrolled. Postsecondary educational opportunities are equally few. Eduardo Mondlane University in Maputo is Mozambique's oldest university. Its roots date back to 1962 when the Portuguese colonial government established the General University Studies of Mozambique (EGUM). At the time EGUM offered only nine courses. EGUM was upgraded to form the University of Lourenco Marques (LUM). However, the institution remained steeped in colonial politics and discriminated against black Mozambicans, a policy that did not end until the attainment of independence. LUM was renamed Eduardo Mondlane University in 1976 in honor of the founding father of Frelimo. The government budgetary allocation for the ministry of education has shown marked increases in recent years to help cope with the demand for education at practically all levels.

Besides the public universities, Mozambique has since the 1990s witnessed the growth of private institutions of higher learning. The Higher Polytechnic and University Institute (ISPU) and the Catholic University of Mozambique (UCM) were established in 1996. The next two years saw the establishment of the Higher Institute of Sciences and Technology of Mozambique (ISCTEM) and the Mussa Bin Bique University (UMBB), in 1997 and 1998 respectively. The development of private universities has been made possible by the transition to a market economy as well as the demand for higher education that has increased due to the government's expansion of educational opportunities at the primary and high-school levels.

The government is also working closely with donors to develop distance learning as a workable alternative. In 1998 the government of Mozambique and the Commonwealth of Learning (COL), which is an intergovernmental organization created by the Commonwealth Heads of Government to encourage the development of distance education, launched the Out of School Secondary Education Pilot Project (OSSE). OSSE's target groups are out-of-school young adults, girls, and women, primary school teachers without secondary education, and district administrative officers. It is hoped that distance learning will help the government in its concerted efforts to increase universal access to education.

RESOURCES, OCCUPATIONS, AND ECONOMY

Mozambique is rich in mineral resources that include natural gas, bauxite, coal, asbestos, gold, mica, and copper. Prospecting for petroleum has not yielded any breakthroughs. Despite the existence of these resources, Mozambique remains one of the poorest countries in the world. This state of underdevelopment is mainly due to the country's colonial past, the civil war that ensued after the attainment of independence, the economic policies pursued by the Frelimo government in the first 15 years of independence, and the persistent occurrence of natural disasters. Despite tremendous accomplishments in recent years that include economic reforms, a marked economic growth rate, and direct foreign investment, the country has yet to realize its full economic potential.

Mozambique was a Portuguese colony. In 1878 Portugal leased large tracts of territory to trading companies who used conscripted African labor to further their economic interests and build infrastructure.[15] The companies had very little regard for African interests, economic or political. Africans were important only as a source of cheap labor. Portugal broke up the trading companies and imposed direct rule over the colony in 1932. The shift from company rule to direct Portuguese colonial control did little to improve the African condition. On the contrary, direct Portuguese control led to the immigration of thousands of new Portuguese settlers to Mozambique. The result was alienation of land by the Portuguese and the subsequent development of a colonial economy that served mainly the interests of settlers. Like most colonies, Portugal practiced the policy of internal protectionism. Portuguese companies were given concessions in trading with Mozambique, and raw materials from the country were shipped to Portugal for processing. The result was an economy that deemphasized industrialization in the colony.[16] The Cabora Bassa hydroelectric power plant was completed in 1974 on the eve of independence. This shows how Mozambique's vast hydroelectric potential remained untapped for most of the colonial period.

The colonial economy was weakened by the liberation war that began in the early 1960s. The war went on for well over a decade. It was characterized by assassinations, reprisals, sabotage, and destruction of infrastructure, both physical and social. The country was in chaos when it attained independence in 1975. It was lacking in skilled professionals and infrastructure, capital was scarce, and the economy plummeted. Frelimo, the governing party under the leadership of Samora Machel, turned to the Soviet Union and East Germany for development aid. In the context of the Cold War this meant the rejection of the West and a market economy and the acceptance of a socialist economy. Frelimo leadership hoped to build a socialist economy based on Marxist-Leninist principles.

Frelimo's economic policies failed to revamp the economy. Instead it led to economic decline and impoverishment of the population.[17] By the end of the Marxist-Leninist economic experiment in the late 1980s, Mozambique was one of the poorest countries in the world. The country was bankrupt, the local currency was worthless, and goods were scarce. A number of factors explain this economic disaster. The government became the dominant power controlling practically all aspects of economic life. Policy pitfalls such as nationalizing means of production led to capital flight, disincentive, and a lack of support from the World Bank and International Monetary Fund. Also, counterrevolutionary insurgencies by the Mozambique National Resistance Movement (Renamo), which was being financed by the South Rhodesian regime (until 1980) and South Africa, undermined any hopes of establishing peace and stability or economic growth.[18] The purpose of the insurgents was to sabotage development projects, alienate the government from the citizenry, and force it to give up power. The road and rail infrastructure were run down as Renamo insurgents constantly destroyed them.

Between 1981 and 1985 the Gross Domestic Product fell by about 8 percent a year, and marketed production of the main agricultural products in 1986 was only about 25 percent of the 1980 level.[19] This grim economic situation forced Frelimo leadership to retreat from socialism in an attempt to reverse the massive decline of the Mozambican economy. In 1989 Frelimo formally abandoned its Marxist-Leninist economic platform that fostered socialist economy. The government embraced political and market economic reforms, including many political parties and the role of private enterprise in the economy. The result of these reforms has been instrumental in Mozambique's marked economic turnaround since 1992.

Mozambique reduced inflation from a high of 70 percent in 1994 to 4 percent in 1999. Foreign exchange stabilized, and the real economic growth rate averaged over 8 percent between 1995 and 1999. It is one of the fastest-growing economies in Africa and one of the highest economic growth rates in the world. The country's economic success has been due to the government's conservative fiscal and monetary policies, civil service reform, reducing budget deficit, tax and expenditure reforms aimed at promoting private sector development, and trade liberalization. The government has reformed the tax system by making it broader by introducing a value-added tax (VAT) and streamlining revenue collection. Mozambique has offered a variety of tax incentives to investors depending on region and type of investment. The private sector's response to these government incentives has been positive.

The private sector is playing a vital role in the rehabilitation and modernization of the infrastructure. The port of Beira, rehabilitated by the Dutch, is one of the best-functioning ports in Mozambique. Cornelder of Netherlands is managing the port under a joint-venture agreement and management concession with CFM Rail Company. In the telephone sector, the state-owned national company (TDM) went into cellular service through a joint venture with Deutsche Telekom. A partnership between the government and the private sector has also been instrumental in the rehabilitation of the nation's road and rail networks. In 1995 the government launched the billion-dollar Maputo Corridor road and rail network, which was aimed at reconnecting South African industrial centers with the Mozambique coast. The completion of the network has facilitated communication between South Africa and

Mozambique by reducing travel time between Maputo and Johannesburg to about five hours.

Despite efforts at industrialization, agriculture remains the most important sector, constituting 34 percent of the GDP. The chief agricultural exports include prawns, cashews, cotton, sugar, copra, citrus, coconuts, and timber. Agriculture provides employment to 81 percent of the population. Despite the significance of agriculture, food insecurity is still a major problem. The 1999 and 2000 floods that destroyed crops and displaced thousands resulted in a major food shortfall. Industry and services provide employment to 6 and 13 percent respectively. Industry constitutes 18 percent of GDP. Minerals being mined include bauxite, gold, mica, and copper. Services contribute 48 percent of the GDP.

Mozambique's weak industrial base means that it has a huge balance of trade. In 1998 exports totaled U.S.$169 million, while imports stood at U.S.$784 million.[20] The country imports farm and transport machinery and equipment as well as petroleum. Prolonged drought and flood occasionally necessitate importing food. The main nonagricultural exports include natural gas and hydroelectric power to the more industrialized South Africa and other neighboring countries.[21]

Local trade is an integral part of the Mozambican economy. People trade in local commodities, mainly agricultural products. Kitchenware from local artisans markets and used clothes are sold in the many open-air markets that dot the rural and urban areas. Other small-scale businesses include hairdressing and car and bicycle repair shops. Local entrepreneurs run inexpensive hotels and restaurants, and this small-scale business sector, which is diverse and strong, offers many job opportunities to the local communities.

Because of its proximity to South Africa, which has a stronger economy, thousands of Mozambicans still cross the border to look for employment there. This is a development that dates to the colonial period, when the need for African labor by mining companies could not be met from within South Africa. This led to the development of migrant wage labor, which gained strength during the civil war in Mozambique when the economy almost ground to a halt. The workers would remit their earnings back to sustain their families who were left behind.

Mozambique is well ahead of other African countries in implementing policies aimed at stimulating economic growth. With the economic instability in Zimbabwe, Mozambique is attracting many investors who are interested in investing in southern Africa. South African firms are also investing in Mozambique because of the sound economic policies that allow for generous tax breaks and repatriation of profits. Nonetheless, Mozambique has a long way to go in modernizing her infrastructure that is still quite basic.[22]

Its railroad network is slightly over 2,000 miles. The total highway mileage is 19,000 miles, out of which only 2,300 is paved. It has 170 airports, out of which only 22 have paved runways. In spite of these challenges, Mozambique has put in place a sound economic framework and an enabling environment that is attracting direct investment as well as a sustained GDP growth rate. The government's poverty eradication strategy, which partly entails increased funding for education and healthcare, has boosted primary school enrolment and expanded access to healthcare.

GOVERNMENT-POLITICAL SYSTEM AND LEGAL SYSTEM

Mozambique is an independent, sovereign, unitary, and democratic republic. The country is a secular state, and the separation between church and state is entrenched in the constitution. The activity of religious institutions is subject to law. The republic, however, recognizes and values religious denominations that promote a climate of social understanding and tolerance and strengthen national unity. As a result all religions—indigenous, Christian, and Islam—operate freely in the country, and Mozambique has avoided the religious conflicts that have characterized some African countries.

According to the 1990 constitution, the executive, the legislature, and the judiciary are separate, and their powers well defined. The president is the chief executive of the republic, is elected directly by the people, and is the head of state and government as well as commander-in-chief of the armed and security forces. A candidate must garner more than 50 percent of the votes cast in the general election to be declared president. His term is limited to three terms of five years each. The president appoints the cabinet, which is convened and chaired by the prime minister, to whom this power is delegated by the president.

The highest legislative body in the Republic of Mozambique is the assembly. It comprises 250 members who are elected by direct universal suffrage and secret personal ballot. Their tenure is unlimited as long as they get reelected every five years. Political parties sponsor candidates for the assembly. Although political pluralism is entrenched in the constitution, no political party may be formed on the basis of religion, ethnicity, or region. This provision is an important safeguard against forming parties that could create religious, ethnic, or regional schism and destabilize the country. In spite of the expansion of democratic space by the 1990 Constitution, Frelimo and Renamo are the two important parliamentary political parties, with the former being the dominant political party, having been in power since independence in 1975. In addition to the two dominant political parties a number of political pressure groups are active and contribute to the vibrant and competitive politics prevalent in the country, including the Institute for Peace and Democracy and the Mozambican League of Human Rights. The major function of the assembly is to make laws and exercise oversight over government functions through its committees.

The judiciary is independent of the executive and the legislature branches. Judges are independent and owe obedience only to the law. The courts are charged with the responsibility of guaranteeing and strengthening the rule of law by safeguarding the fundamental rights of citizens. The Supreme Court is the highest court in the country. It acts as a trial court of original as well as appellate jurisdiction. The president appoints 7 judges, including the chief justice of the Supreme Court, while the assembly elects 17 judges.

HISTORY

Early History

Bantu-speaking groups moved into the present day Mozambique toward the end of the first millennium. The migration was part of the Bantu migration into southern Africa. The Bantu were agriculturalists and lived in nucleated settlements. They established cities along the east coast and traded with India and Arabia. Swahili was widely spoken along the coast. It was the language of international commerce between Eastern Africa and Arabia. African traders acted as middlemen between the hinterland communities and the Arab traders at the coast who financed the trade. Islam was widely practiced in the coastal settlements. The result was a politically stable and thriving coastal region whose hinterland extended into much of what is today central Africa.

Kingdoms and States

Sofala was the preeminent city-state of commerce and administration since the ninth century. It was under the leadership of a sheikh. The sheikh was invariably an Arab and claimed kinship with ruling families of other East African coastal city-states. He practiced the Islamic faith and levied tribute on items imported and exported through Sofala. Ivory, cotton cloth, and gold were the most significant items of trade from the region. However, items such as gold and ivory came from the interior. Sofala was only significant to the extent that it was the major port and financiers of the trade coordinated their hinterland commercial activities from the city.

The Mozambican plateau was the home to many kingdoms and states dating from the eleventh through the seventeenth century. The Shona founded one such empire during the eleventh century.[23] The empire occupied the greater part of the modern territory of Zimbabwe, including the area between the Sabi and Pungwe rivers down to the Indian Ocean in modern Mozambique.

The wealth of the empire was derived from its control of long-distance trade route between the gold-producing reefs to the north and the west and Sofala on the Indian Ocean. The rulers of Shona rewarded their supporters from the tribute they collected in ivory, gold, and food. They increased their power and attracted many artisans who worked gold and copper into fine jewelry. The decline of the Shona empire was caused by many factors including emigration, a degraded environment, and the rise of the Monomotapa kingdom to the northeast in the first half of the fifteenth century.[24]

By the 1480s the Monomotapa kingdom had expanded eastwards into the Mozambican coastal lowlands. The kingdom had a formidable military that enabled it to maintain control over its subject peoples. The states of Batwe, Ureve, and Manyika were incorporated into the kingdom.[25] They had their own source of alluvial gold, which came from the Mazoe region. The kingdom maintained good relations with the Arab and Swahili traders and used their gold in foreign trade with Arabs and Swahilis to purchase beads, colored cloth, and other luxuries for the country's rulers. It is against this backdrop that the Portuguese sought to replace the Arab and Swahili traders by taking over their forts in the interior while on the other hand forging close links with Monomotapa leadership.

In the early nineteenth century Mozambique was heavily impacted by the Ngoni invasions from the south. The Ngoni, a subgroup of the Northern Nguni, was forced to flee from the south by the Mfecane upheaval.[26] A major revolutionary war, Mfecane was spearheaded by Shaka, king of the Zulu. Thousands of people were displaced, and offshoots from the major turmoil left the region heading towards the north and west. Thus in the 1820s Soshangane, a warlord from northern Nguni, in what is present-day South Africa, invaded southern Mozambique and founded the Gaza kingdom. Soshangane introduced into southern Mozambique an entirely new concept of centralized military organization typical of Shaka's army. The consequence of the upheaval was the widespread use of age-regiments and conscription as major features of political mobilization and organization during the first half of the nineteenth century.

Portuguese Rule and Colonial Order

Portugal was one of the European countries that became interested in reaching India through the southern tip of Africa in order to control trade with the East. The first Portuguese to reach the Mozambican coast was Vasco da Gama in 1498.[27] His main focus was on India, and Mozambique was significant only to the extent that it lay on the route to India and could be used as a supply point. Soon after this initial contact, the Portuguese realized that it was important to control the Mozambican coast as well. This change was motivated by two main factors. First, the Portuguese wanted to control the trade in ivory and gold. The Arab and Swahili traders who dominated the commerce along the East African coast had to be subdued if the Portuguese were to keep the supply points open.

In the interior the Portuguese sought to control the Africans, but not to replace them as middlemen. Their institutions were also retained. However, they were required to recognize Portugal as the new dominant power. This development did not sit well with Arab and Swahili traders who wanted to maintain their control of the East African coastal trade. This led to conflict between the Portuguese on the one hand and the Swahili and Arabs on the other. The result was incessant warfare, which came to characterize the East African coast for much of the sixteenth century. Nevertheless, Portugal had by the end of that century succeeded in supplanting Arab and Swahili traders as the dominant power. They took over several Arab and Swahili trading posts on the banks of the Zambezi and built more at Sena, Tete, and Chikova. By the close of the sixteenth century Portugal had attained its commercial objectives of controlling trade routes to the gold-producing areas in the Mozambican hinterland.[28]

Mozambique became a major slave-trading center in the eighteenth century. This involvement went through various stages influenced by demand. The French needed slave labor to work on their sugar and coffee plantations in Mauritius and Reunion.[29] Initially, the French bought slaves from Portuguese and Indian traders in the Zambezi valley, at Quelimane and at Mozambique. High mortality rates, harsh conditions, and overwork against the backdrop of expanding plantations created a demand for more slaves. In order to meet this demand the French turned to Arab and Swahili traders in East Africa, especially in the Kilwa and Zanzibar markets. They also sponsored slave expeditions into the Mozambican hinterland. Some African traders were enlisted to help in the capture of slaves. The Yao became major suppliers of slaves.

As the era of slave trade drew to a close in the nineteenth century, slaves for sale became scarce. The shortage increased the price of slaves in the Americas. This made the trade lucrative but risky. The link between the Portuguese and Brazilian trade became strong. The higher profit margin made it worthwhile for Brazilian slavers to make the extra-long trip to get slaves from the Indian Ocean coast. Most of the slaves came from Mozambique and the Zambezi valley. Even though Portugal outlawed slave trade from Mozambique in 1842, clandestine trade continued for decades.

The Portuguese control of the territory of what is today Mozambique was anything but effective, particularly from the 1600s well into the first half of the twentieth century. Their control was fragile and mainly confined to forts and trading posts along the coast of the Indian Ocean and the Zambezi River, which was their main route to the interior. This lack of effectiveness was due to two factors. First, the Portuguese did not establish an efficient local administration. They appointed the governor general of Goa in India to administer Mozambique. The Portuguese government was thus distant and far removed from the people.

The second reason was Portugal's decision to grant land concessions (*prazos*) to her subjects.[30] Once granted, the leaders of these prazos, prazeros, were entrusted with full control of the possessions. The prazos gradually began to operate as effective chieftancies accountable to the Portuguese governor general for the general administration and economy of areas under their jurisdiction.[31] However, in the course of several centuries the prazos became increasingly autonomous, and the prazeros resisted Portuguese attempts at imposing direct control over them during the scramble and partition of Africa in the closing decade of the nineteenth century.[32] In 1891 Portugal and Britain defined Mozambique's western and southern borders. With the demarcation of boundaries complete, the Portuguese proceeded to assert direct and effective control. Lourenco Marques, present-day Maputo, became the colonial capital in 1902. Like other European colonial powers, Portugal waged various pacification wars during the first two decades of the twentieth century. In 1917 Portugal suppressed the Barue revolt, which was coordinated by spirit mediums against Portuguese colonial rule. In spite of pacification wars, effective and direct control of the territorial domain of Mozambique was realized in 1932 when Portugal abolished prazos and imposed direct rule over the colony.

The colonial economy in Mozambique evolved and developed as a dependency of the neighboring colonial economies of southern and central Africa. The development of the railroad infrastructure served the interests of the neighboring British colonies more than those of Mozambique itself. Forced labor, low pay, and poor working conditions forced many people to flee the country in search of perceived better pay in the neighboring countries. The demand for labor was quite strong in the neighboring British colonies where there were more settler farms as well as the labor-intensive mining industry, especially in South Africa. Mozambicans who lived in the southern part of the country went to work in the gold mines of South Africa. In the same vein those who lived in the northern and western parts of the country went to work in the mines and settler plantations in Zimbabwe, Malawi, and Zambia. The outflow of migrant labor from Mozambique to the neighboring countries is a manifestation of the weakness of the Mozambican colonial economy.

Transition to Independence

The period after World War II saw serious efforts by Portugal to develop a more vibrant colonial economy based on plantation agriculture. New

Portuguese settlers migrated to Mozambique. The number of settlers in the country more than doubled from 90,000 in the prewar period to more than 200,000 by the 1960s. More land had to be alienated for European settlement. Forced labor intensified as more Africans were put to work on the settler plantations. Rebellion in rural areas and strikes gained momentum in the late 1950s and early 1960s. The colonial economy marginalized Africans. The African elite was denied equal opportunity in employment. Rank and pay were not based on merit, contrary to what they were made to believe. The African elite as well as masses resented Portuguese rule. Despite their ethnic, economic, and political differences, Mozambicans were united by one common cause: liberating their country.

To further their agenda of attaining independence, the African elite founded the Mozambique Liberation Front (Frelimo) in 1962 under the leadership of Eduardo Mondlane. The leadership was convinced that independence could be attained only through diplomacy backed by the use of force. Armed struggle was inevitable. The liberation movement began to prepare for war. In 1963 Frelimo sent its first batch of 250 recruits to Algeria for military training. Algeria had attained independence from France the previous year after one of the longest and bloodiest liberation wars ever fought in Africa. The Mozambican war of liberation was launched in 1964.

Frelimo faced an uphill task. It lacked weapons, faced internal squabbles, and lacked organizational structure. But it had the will and determination to bring down Portuguese rule. As the Portuguese colonial government waged brutal counterinsurgency measures it forced many people to join the liberation movement. The neighboring states of Zambia and Tanzania, under the leadership of Kenneth Kaunda and Julius Nyerere, respectively, provided the Frelimo guerillas with bases from which to wage attacks against the Portuguese colonial government. As the war intensified the Portuguese mined roads, destroyed villages, resorted to assassinations, and arrested thousands of people perceived to be sympathetic to the liberation movement. The purpose of these counterinsurgency measures was to deny the freedom fighters any sanctuary and support from within the country. The Frelimo leader Eduardo Mondlane was assassinated in 1969. One of his closest associates, Samora Machel, was chosen to replace him. Machel soon proved to be an outstanding strategist and brilliant field commander.

The Portuguese counterinsurgency measures as well as assassinations proved counterproductive. The liberation movement gained in numbers and the leadership became more resolute and determined. Portugal was finding it difficult to maintain thousands of troops in Mozambique. Furthermore, the Portuguese colonies of Angola and Guinea Bissau were also fighting liberation wars. As the cost of the war continued to escalate, human casualties mounted on both sides. In sum, the cost of the liberation wars was adversely impacting Portugal. These realities began to be a factor in Portugal's domestic politics.

A military coup in Lisbon in 1974 put power in the hands of National Salvation headed by General Antonio de Spinola. The new government moved swiftly to end the stalemate in the Portuguese African possessions by supporting autonomy for colonies. Portugal and Frelimo signed an accord in Lusaka, Zambia, that set in motion the process of decolonization by establishing a transitional government. The liberation war, one of the longest and bloodiest in Africa, which had led to the deaths of thousands on both sides, the displacement of millions, and near collapse of the economy, drew to a close. Mozambique became independent in 1975 under the leadership of Samora Machel. The Portuguese settlers in Mozambique were devastated. They saw the decision by the National Salvation government to grant independence to Mozambique as an act of betrayal. Many of the settlers left Mozambique at independence. They rejected requests from Frelimo that they should stay to help with the reconstruction efforts and the building of a united nonracial Mozambique.

Civil War

Independence brought anything but stability. Instead, the next two decades of the postindependence period were characterized by brutal civil war between Frelimo and Renamo insurgents. Renamo, an anti-Frelimo resistance group, was formed in 1976. Renamo was from the very beginning patronized by both the South African apartheid and South Rhodesian regimes.[33] The latter feared the rise of another independent African state sympathetic to the African nationalist movements that were fighting to liberate their country from white minority rule, while the former financed Renamo for similar reasons because it was facing liberation fighters who wanted to bring down the regime. The Frelimo leadership also pursued an ideological path that was opposed to Western brand of capitalism and democracy.

Frelimo leadership emphasized a unitary socialist state based on Marxist-Leninist principles. It opposed the apartheid regime in South Africa. As a result of Frelimo's ideological platform and active opposition to the Afrikaner regime, South Africa became actively involved in directing insurgency against the Frelimo government. The Afrikaner regime worked closely with Renamo by financing its operations and sabotaging Frelimo's development projects by destroying physical infrastructure such as roads, bridges, and railroads. Many rural areas were heavily mined, and thousands of people were blown up, while many more lost their limbs. Neighboring states such as Zambia, Tanzania, and Zimbabwe (after her independence in 1980) provided military assistance to Mozambique in order to help stem the insurgency by Renamo and South Africa. As the civil war took its toll on the country, life became insecure, economic life was disrupted, and millions of people were uprooted and fled into exile. At the height of the liberation war in 1974 Mozambique had 250,000 refugees. This number had increased to 1.7 million by 1992-93, at the end of the civil war, while those displaced within Mozambique stood at nearly 4 million.[34]

As military and economic pressure mounted on Frelimo, the country's economy almost ground to a halt by the early 1980s, and the local currency almost collapsed. Basic commodities such as oil and sugar were hard to come by. Renamo and the Afrikaner regime in South Africa had succeeded in making the Mozambique government politically unstable and economically vulnerable. Samora Machel began to mend fences with the Western countries in an attempt to salvage the country's economy. He also proceeded to negotiate with the apartheid regime. As a result, Machel signed a pact, the Nkomati Accord, with Pik Botha, president of apartheid South Africa, on March 16, 1984.[35] According to the Nkomati Accord, the Mozambican government was to stop providing sanctuary to the South African nationalist movements, especially the African National Congress. The apartheid regime was to cease military assistance to Renamo. The accord did not end the hostilities. Instead, civil war continued to rage for the next eight years. Unfortunately, Samora Machel died in an airplane crash on October 19, 1986. Joachim Chissano, one of the inner group of Frelimo leaders, succeeded him.

President Chissano took office against the backdrop of civil war, an ailing economy, and a hostile apartheid South Africa.[36] He maintained a hard stance against Renamo because of atrocities perpetrated by the movement and began to strengthen links with the Western countries by building on the foundation laid by his predecessor. The situation in southern Africa began to change in the late 1980s as a result of the end of the Cold War and F. W. DeKlerk's accession to power as the president of apartheid South Africa. Socialism based on Marxist-Leninist principles was discredited. Frelimo formally abandoned its commitment to the Marxist-Leninist ideology as the basis for development in 1989, and the country began to embrace economic and political reforms.

In neighboring South Africa DeKlerk instituted reforms and lifted the ban on the African National Congress. Apartheid South Africa's support for Renamo waned. These global, regional, and internal developments emboldened the reformers in Frelimo to push for a more liberal economy, a new constitution, normalization of relations with the Western countries, and a peace initiative with Renamo. A new constitution was promulgated in 1990, ending the de jure one-party rule that had characterized Mozambique since 1977. It allowed for political pluralism and multiparty elections. International mediators capitalized on these positive developments to broker peace between

Frelimo and Renamo. A cease-fire agreement was signed on October 15, 1992. This marked the formal end of the civil war.

Since the end of civil war, Mozambique has moved to ensure political stability and economic development. Political pluralism is entrenched in the constitution, and competitive parliamentary elections are held regularly. In 1994, 1999, and 2004 competitive multiparty elections were held. President Chissano emerged victorious in the first two elections and retired at the end of his term in 2004. The Frelimo party won the 2004 elections under the leadership of Armando Gueburza. However, the main opposition party, Renamo, has gained in strength in parliament. In spite of having fewer members of parliament than Frelimo, it cannot be taken for granted in legislative matters. The Frelimo government has moved to revamp its once stagnant economy. The government published its Strategy for Poverty Reduction in 1995. The strategy set out for the first time explicit policies for poverty reduction in the country. The country now attracts direct foreign investment. In 1999 the boards of the International Development Association and International Monetary Fund agreed to a set of significant enhancements to help Mozambique reduce its debt burden and help facilitate economic growth. The country was one of the first less-developed countries to be given debt relief. Mozambique has put in place structures as well as incentives that have been instrumental in attracting direct foreign investment. As a result of working with the international financial institutions and humanitarian aid agencies, Mozambique is poised to be one of the most economically stable countries in the region in the not too distant future. It has one of the fastest-growing economies in Africa, averaging well over five percent in the last couple of years. Furthermore, the country has gone through peaceful multiparty elections since peace was restored following the cessation of civil war. This does not mean that the country is without major developmental challenges. Providing education, healthcare, infrastructure, and a diversified economy are some of the issues that the government is grappling with.

NOTES

1. United States of America, "CIA World Factbook: Mozambique," https://www.cia.gov/cia/publications/factbook/geos/mz.html (2005).

2. USA, "CIA World Factbook: Mozambique."

3. USA, "CIA World Factbook: Mozambique."

4. USA, "CIA World Factbook: Mozambique."

5. USA, "CIA World Factbook: Mozambique."

6. F. James Ramsay, *Global Studies: Africa* (Guildford, CT: Dushkin/McGraw Hill, 1999), 152.

7. Margaret Hall and Tom Young, *Confronting Leviathan: Mozambique since Independence* (Athens: Ohio University Press, 1997).

8. William Finnegan, *A Complicated War: The Harrowing of Mozambique* (Berkeley: University of California Press, 1992).

9. Hall and Young, *Confronting Leviathan,* 189–234.

10. Edward A. Alpers, *Ivory and Slaves in East Central Africa: Changing Patterns of International Trade to the Later Nineteenth Century* (London: Heinemann, 1975).

11. Malyn Newitt, *A History of Mozambique* (Bloomington and Indianapolis: Indiana University Press, 1995), 256–266.

12. Newitt, *A History of Mozambique,* 438–441.

13. Hall and Young, *Confronting Leviathan,* 56.

14. United Nations Educational, Social, and Cultural Organization, "Education for All: Report of Mozambique," http://www2.unesco.org/wet/countryreports/mozambique/contents.html (2003).

15. Newitt, *A History of Mozambique.*

16. Newitt, *A History of Mozambique,* 453–459, 468–470.

17. Merle L. Bowen, *The State against the Peasantry: Rural Struggles in Colonial and Postcolonial Mozambique* (Charlottesville: University of Virginia Press, 2000).

18. John S. Saul, *Recolonization and Resistance: Southern Africa in the 1990s* (Trenton, NJ: Africa World Press, 1993).

19. Hall and Young, *Confronting Leviathan,* 196.

20. Ramsay, *Africa,* 152.

21. Ramsay, *Africa,* 152.

22. Ramsay, *Africa,* 152.

23. Newitt, *A History of Mozambique,* 31–49.

24. S. I. Mudenge, *A Political History of Munhumutapa* (Harare, Zimbabwe: Zimbabwe Publishing House, 1986).

25. Newitt, *A History of Mozambique,* 44–45.

26. John Wright, "Mfecane," in Kevin Shillington, ed., *Encyclopedia of African History* (New York/London: Fitzroy Dearborn Publishers, 2005), 979–980.

27. R. S. James, *Places and Peoples of the World: Mozambique* (New York and Philadelphia: Chelsea House Publishers, 1988), 15.

28. Erik Gilbert and Jonathan T. Reynolds, *Africa in World History* (Upper Saddle River, NJ: Pearson/Prentice Hall, 2004), 204–205.

29. Newitt, *A History of Mozambique,* 244–245.

30. Newitt, *A History of Mozambique,* 217–242.

31. Newitt, *A History of Mozambique,* 337–340.

32. Allen F. Isaacman, *Mozambique: The Africanization of a European Institution, the Zambezi Prazos, 1750–1902* (Madison: University of Wisconsin Press, 1972).

33. Hall and Young, *Confronting Leviathan,* 125–130.

34. Mario Joaquim Azevedo, *Tragedy and Triumph: Mozambique Refugees in South Africa, 1977–2001* (Portsmouth, NH: Heinemann, 2002).

35. Hall and Young, *Confronting Leviathan,* 146.

36. Barry Munslow, "Mozambique after Machel," *Third World Quarterly* 10, 1 (1988): 23–26.

2

Religion and Worldview

RELIGION IS AN INTEGRAL part of Mozambican societal life. All communities in Mozambique profess belief in the existence of a supreme being. As a result, religious ideas and worldview play an instrumental role in the way Mozambicans relate to their environment, define interpersonal relations, and communicate with God. The existence of various religions in Mozambique has broadened and influenced Mozambicans' worldview. In addition to traditional religion, many Mozambicans have successfully embraced and domesticated Islam and Christianity. Yet in the process of this embrace and acceptance, they still retain certain core values that define them as a people, a culture, and a society.

Mozambicans worship in churches or mosques, while at the same time they are quite comfortable with their customary law that is rooted in traditional society. Children attend formal schools, but they are still expected to exhibit honor and respect and maintain the intergenerational communication that was at the very core of traditional education. In sum, Mozambicans are open to ideas from various religious strands, but the tendency is to domesticate those influences so that society can modernize without losing the traditional values of tolerance and accommodation, humaneness, and an attitude and behavior that are not rigid or fixed, but are based on history and evolving experience. It is against this backdrop that this chapter explores the role of religion in Mozambican society with specific reference to the origins, evolution, and development of various religious traditions in contemporary Mozambique.

Mozambican communities practiced traditional religion long before the coming of either Islam or Christianity. They had a clear concept of God as the creator and giver of life. God was worshipped and praised. People sacrificed to God. The mode of worship, praise, and sacrifice varied from one community to another. The other two major religions—Islam and Christianity— are not indigenous to Mozambique.

The Arabs brought Islam to Mozambique via trade. The East African coast, Arabian peninsula, and Southwest Asia were linked together by the Indian Ocean in a commercial network that saw not only the exchange of commodities and ideas, but also culture. By 700 A.D. Arabs were visiting the coast of Mozambique. As Arabs increasingly got involved in this trade, a number of them began to establish a presence along the East African coast to control the trade. By around 1000 A.D. Arabs had established trading posts all along the Mozambican coast. Sofala grew to become the preeminent center of trade on the East African coast. Mosques were built for the immigrants from Arabia as well as for African converts to the Islamic faith. Islam's influence was confined to the northeastern coastal part of Mozambique.

The Portuguese brought Christianity to Mozambique during the early fifteenth century. Vasco da Gama circumnavigated Africa and reached India in 1498. Subsequent to this development, the Portuguese made considerable efforts to establish their presence on the east coast of Africa as a way of securing their interests by protecting the sea route to India. Portugal established a settlement at the site of present-day Beira in 1505. Two years later, they established a fort on Mozambique Island. The Christian communities in these forts comprised a core of Portuguese, a larger number of mesticos (persons of mixed Portuguese and African parentage), and Africans. The number of Christians in the forts was usually in the hundreds. The Christian leadership was invariably European and Roman Catholic, either of Dominican or Jesuit order.

Protestant groups reached Mozambique in the nineteenth century. The first successful and enduring Protestant missionaries came from South Africa largely as a result of initiatives by Africans who had been converted to Protestant churches. Interaction between the people of Mozambique and South Africa intensified as a result of the mineral revolution beginning in the 1880s. The exploitation of minerals required labor, which was drawn from the entire southern African region. As migrant labor moved to and from South Africa, some embraced Protestantism and spread it in Mozambique. As time wore on a number of Protestant missions were established in the country, but Roman Catholicism remained the predominant church in the country.

The Christian churches were instrumental in promoting Western education in colonial Mozambique. The churches established schools and mission stations where Africans were taught literacy skills as well as catechism. Although there were few schools vis-à-vis the number of children, these institutions helped to produce a small Mozambican elite that served the church as catechists and the colonial government as teachers, nurses, and clerks. These elite also constituted the leadership of the liberation movement that was instrumental in dismantling Portuguese colonialism in Mozambique.

In spite of the Church's role in promoting literacy, the partnership between the Roman Catholic Church and the state compromised the ability of the Church to speak up against the ills of Portuguese colonialism in Mozambique. The state patronized the Roman Catholic Church, and the two became indistinguishable in promoting colonial policies that adversely impacted the lives of the Africans. Unusually few church leaders spoke up against such policies. During the liberation war that sought to free Mozambique, the Portuguese resorted to brutal counterinsurgency measures that resulted in the destruction of whole villages and the deaths of thousands of Africans. These extreme fascist measures led the Church leadership in Mozambique to break ranks with the state and condemn the atrocities perpetrated by the colonial authorities.

This chapter examines two main issues. First it delves into the significance of the traditional religion and worldview, its basic outlines and its influential role in societal life. The chapter also examines the complex role of nonindigenous religions in Mozambican society against the backdrop of the history of religious traditions, their interactions, and how such interactions have been instrumental in shaping Mozambican contemporary culture, politics, education, and economy.

TRADITIONAL RELIGIONS

A majority of Mozambicans practice traditional religions. Most of the ethnic religions are not animistic, as is usually claimed. The fact that these religions are distinct from Christianity and Islam does not make them animistic. Their adherents do not worship nature. Instead, they see nature as the handiwork and manifestation of the Supreme Being. The Tonga and the Shona hold the view that storms are God's manifestations, while lightning is the instrument by which he punishes people or accomplishes intentions. Among the Yao and neighboring communities mist is believed to be sent by God to protect crops from the scorching heat of the sun, while the Venda hold the view that a thunderstorm is a manifestation of God's presence when he comes to make his wishes to the chief.[1] A distinction is made between God and the instruments through which he acts.

Natural calamities such as flood, famine, drought, and lightning are considered happenings out of the ordinary. Their occurrence evokes a plethora of explanations ranging from a manifestation of God's power to displeasure by him or departed ancestors at an individual, family, clan, or community for some violation of societal moral prescriptions. The supremacy of God, and his omnipotence and omnipresence, are not questioned. Thus, a common thread that runs through these beliefs is that natural phenomenon are the means through which God communicates his message, manifests his power, and exercises control over humankind.

God in the traditional Mozambican religions is described as the creator and maker of the universe. Human life began with God, continues in God, and ends with God. There are personal, family, and community prayers. An individual can say prayers to thank God or to seek assistance from God. The head of the family, usually an elder, conducts family prayers. However, community prayers are usually led by a traditional priest or diviner on occasions that are of community interest such as during good harvests or initiation ceremonies, which marked important developmental stages in one's life such as birth, circumcision, marriage, and death; outbreaks of war; or prolonged drought. Individual prayers are primarily for personal needs, family ones are for familial matters, and community prayers are for community-oriented interests.

The Yao assert that God, *Mulungu,* is the Supreme Being and creator. Mulungu embodies the spirit of all human beings that is formed by adding all the spirits of the departed together.[2] The Yao further believe that Mulungu predestined the state of both men and spirits. The Makua portray their God, *Muluku,* in similar terms: a creator that made the earth. As the creator, protector, and life giver, God is praiseworthy and thankworthy. Prayer constitutes an integral part of people's communication with their God.

The Makonde too pray to God on various occasions. In the morning they pray: "We rise up in the morning before the day, to betake ourselves to our labor, to prepare our harvest. Protect us from the dangerous animal and from the serpent, and from every stumbling block."[3] For a bountiful harvest the Makonde thank God and seek further blessings in the next year: "May our grain bear so much fruit that it be forgotten on the ground and that it lets fall along the path so much that next year when we go forth to seed, the fields and the pathways will be covered with grain."[4] During war, Makonde prayers seek God's intervention on their side: "Our enemies approach. God, fortify our arms, grant us strength."[5] Before a cattle raid the Makonde offer this prayer:[6]

Leader (recites):	Other People (respond)
Let us say to God:	
Grant us many cattle!	He will grant it.
Grant us life!	He will grant it.

Grant us health and happiness!	He will grant it.
Grant us victory!	He will grant it.
Grant us much booty!	He will grant it.

People turn to God on many other occasions such as during victory, birth, initiation, and weddings. In all the prayers pertaining to these events, God's supremacy over his creation is acknowledged and praised.

Followers of traditional religion place themselves in the midst of time with a view to understanding their positions in a growing and changing society. They see religion as a set of beliefs that seeks to explain the ultimate questions of reality, the nature of the world, and humanity, as well as a way and means of addressing humanity's primary challenges such as illness, suffering, and death. The basic and fundamental concern for Mozambican traditional religions is to overcome crisis in the present life as well as the apocalyptic epoch of human beings' separation from God. The communities seek to explain the mortality of human beings and the end of life. They also seek peace and oneness with God. A Mozambican's worldview is thus closely linked to religion.

All the communities in Mozambique have myths that depict their origin and subsequent separation from God because of the intransigence of human beings. The Yao narrative of how their separation from God came about best expresses this genre of myths. The Yao believe that God dwelt here on earth with human beings before they learned to make fire by friction. Shortly after the innovation, they set grasslands ablaze. God then withdrew himself to heaven and ordered that henceforth human beings must go where he is after death where they will serve him as his servants.[7]

Such myths are not insignificant. They are in many ways used to sanctify the beliefs and place them beyond questions. The message is clear: God loves humankind, and the separation is temporary because eventually he expects his people to be with him in heaven after death, which is a form of atonement for misconduct. Despite prayer and sacrifice, intransigence on the part of human beings brought death and marked the end of original direct contact and relationship between God and humankind. In a sense, traditional religions offer a vision of hope and survival through an integrated approach of explaining natural phenomenon.

Traditional religions represent a culture into which individuals are born and nurtured. One is born into a culture and is bound by it from birth to well after death. The individual has no exit option. There are rituals and ceremonies that mark the birth of a child and the initiation from childhood to adulthood, marriage, and death. All these are part and parcel of traditional religion. The secular and religious are one and coexist without any conflict. A person finds fulfillment in being a member of family, lineage, clan, and community. The individual's identity is in reference to the community. As a result, the community sets moral prescriptions and good conduct. Human beings must always strive to adhere to the moral prescriptions and orderly conduct established by society. Failure to adhere to such established norms could result in one being chastised, condemned, or ostracized by the community. It is believed that individual misconduct could bring pain and suffering not only to the individual, but also to the entire family, lineage, and community. The community is therefore forced to ensure strict compliance to the prescribed moral precepts or face the wrath of God and ancestors.

Ancestors are highly regarded in the traditional Mozambican religions. They are not worshipped, but are seen as intermediaries between the living and God. Their names are evoked during prayers—personal, familial, or communal. Ancestral spirits are praised and appealed to for intercession on behalf of the living so that God can respond to the requests asked of him. The ancestral spirits are offered libations, offerings, and sacrifices so that they can look favorably on the living and intercede on their behalf during times of distress. As a result, appeasing God and the departed ancestors is undertaken to ensure that peace prevails and calamities are prevented from occurring. This is done by promoting chastity, fidelity, and societal cohesion as per the societal moral prescription and by making offerings to God and the ancestors.

However, not all spirits are associated with ancestors. God is believed to have created some of them, while others are personifications of natural objects and phenomenon. The major distinction among the three types is that most of the ancestral ones tend to be friendly and receptive to human requests. They were once human beings who lived and produced children. Their children and grandchildren in due course formed lineages and clans. While physically they are gone, the connection is not lost. It is believed that they look with favor on their descendants to ensure that they live their lives to the fullest and subject to the dictates of the society. In that way, their names are often evoked and their memories kept alive. A few ancestral spirits are unfriendly and torment the living. These are usually believed to be the spirits of those who were witches. Also, those who were neglected in life and died in bitterness as well as those who are unhappy that ceremonies to honor them in death were not conducted fall under the category of bad spirits. Similarly, those who committed suicide belong to this category. Because they are angry and bitter, bad spirits do not wish the living well.

That traditional worldview and religion are closely linked is best illustrated by the fact that illness is attributed to multiple factors that include natural and supernatural causes. This calls for myriad solutions including medical and psychotherapeutic remedies. Traditional medical practitioners understand this quite well and use a wide array of herbal medicines as well as psychological treatment. Successful medical practitioners are ones who can combat witchcraft, exorcise demons, administer herbal medicine, psychologically stabilize the patient, and be reassuring that all will be well. Traditional healers are pragmatic and know that they operate in a defined worldview and religious context. They have to capture the mind and win the confidence of the patient for the healing of the physical body to be effective.

It is not uncommon to find a Mozambican consulting a traditional healer, while at the same time visiting a mainstream modern healthcare facility. There appears to be no conflict because of the belief that modern healthcare is significantly better than traditional healthcare in many ways, but yet still is unable to offer explanations pertaining to the many mysteries of illnesses or causes of death to satisfy the many who still value their traditional worldview. There is a lack of modern healthcare facilities in rural areas where the majority of Mozambicans live. This has led many people to depend on the traditional healers. It is important to point out that the effectiveness of the traditional medicine is not in doubt. Many Mozambicans see the two systems as complementary and not in conflict.

Besides traditional healers, various communities have other specialists. There are spirit mediums, leaders whose primary function is to link the living and the ancestors by communicating messages from the latter in order to predict some impending disaster or advise the community on what to do to prevent such an occurrence from taking place. Ritual leaders are equally important in leading people during rituals such as marriage, initiation, or the burial of notable leaders of the community. The various specialists, medicine men, spirit mediums, ritual leaders, and rainmakers all have one underlying and important function: to transmute the immediacy of pain and sorrow, tragedy and suffering in human life into a spiritual and physical health that yields peace and order for self, family, and community.

The foregoing traditional worldview and religions, including accompanying practices, apply across Mozambique and demonstrate the core principles espoused by various communities. Chastity, spirituality, and living as a member of community are values that characterize all Mozambican communities. There may be slight differences in the way in which specific communities conduct their rituals and deal with moral lapses, but these do not contradict core beliefs and assumptions pertaining to God, spirituality, moral uprightness, ancestors, death, and afterlife. Also, because tradition is a historical movement, localized in time, space, and ethnicity, it is subject to change, albeit over a long period of time. Traditional religion has not been immune to a number of forces, the dominant three of which are Christianity, Westernization, and Islam.

CHRISTIANITY

Christianity reached Mozambique in the opening decades of the sixteenth century. The first Christian denomination was Roman Catholic. At the time, the long-term Portuguese presence in Mozambique was in doubt because their primary preoccupation was to secure India for economic considerations. The nascent Christian community was established to take care of the spiritual needs of the Portuguese, Mesticos, and Africans. The converts were few and numbered only in the hundreds. This Christian community was graced by a number of renowned leaders of the Roman Catholic Church. The most notable of them all was Saint Francis Xavier of the Jesuit order, who spent six months in Mozambique in 1541 while on his way to Goa in India where the archdiocese headquarters was based.[8] Before 1560 Christianity was largely confined to the coastal region. None of the missionaries ventured deep into the hinterland.

From the middle of the sixteenth century, Portuguese pioneers began to venture into the Mozambican hinterland. The purpose of this venture was to find gold in the fabled Mwene Mutapa kingdom.[9] The Portuguese sent military expeditions to pacify the hinterland communities and access and control the fabled gold mines. It had little to do with the spread of Christianity. This led to hostility against any Portuguese who ventured into the interior. It is against this backdrop that Goncalo da Silveira, a Jesuit priest who reached the court of the Mutapa king in 1561, met with a hostile reception and was subsequently killed.[10] With such initial setbacks, Portuguese political influence and economic centers remained largely confined to the Sena and Tete regions adjacent to the coast, regions where pockets of Islamic influence existed.[11] Evangelization too remained confined to the two main regions in the period before the seventeenth century.

Mozambique became an independent diocese in 1612. This, however, did not de-link the diocese from the king of Portugal, because the two continued to work closely together. The significance of the independence, though, lies in the fact that the Church in Mozambique became more aggressive and focused on the evangelization of local populations. In this regard, the two orders that were instrumental in the evangelization process were the Dominicans and the Jesuits. The Dominicans concentrated their missionary work on the people in the interior, while the Jesuits focused on the Tonga people along the Zambezi valley. The result of these missionary initiatives failed to yield significant results in the number of converts until the period after the middle of the seventeenth century. Subsequent to that period a major development that resulted in the increased number of converts was the slave trade—slaves were baptized before they were exported.

As the number of slaves for export increased in the eighteenth and nineteenth centuries, the demand for baptizing equally surged. To meet the demand, the missionaries resorted to a hasty method of mass baptisms. The baptized were given Christian/European names. But herein lies a paradox: The missionaries failed to condemn slave trade; they endorsed and participated in it. This meant that the very people who sanctioned the slaves' capture and subsequent enslavement baptized them as they converted them.

The partnership between the slave traders and the missionaries was not without reason. The missionaries, both Dominicans and Jesuits, held a number of estates, *prazos*. Those who lived and worked on the prazos were either tenants or slaves. The missionaries needed African labor to work on their prazos just as the slave traders needed African slaves to work on their plantations outside of Mozambique and for sale to other groups for profit. Shared economic interests trumped the gospel message of equality, humanity, and love. The Catholic Church in Mozambique connived with the state to sacrifice human value, freedom, and decency at the altar of profits and racial brotherhood. The result was the love/hate relationship between the Africans and the Roman Catholics in Mozambique. The Catholics presented the gospel message of love, compassion, and hope, while in the same vein they participated in the very ills that their gospel message condemned.

However, the relationship between the Catholic Church in Mozambique and the Portuguese colonial state was not always cordial. In 1759 the king of Portugal ordered the Jesuits in the Portuguese possessions of Mozambique and Angola arrested and deported.[12] Their property was also to be sold. The order was a direct result of the disagreement between the king and the Vatican. It led to the persecution of Jesuits not only in Mozambique, but also in many other Portuguese possessions abroad. The withdrawal of the Jesuits adversely impacted the growth of the Church in Mozambique as the number of missionaries and the institutions of the Church declined sharply. The Church continued to exist in Mozambique, but its influence as well as partnership with the state was eroded. The Jesuits returned in the late nineteenth century, but were again expelled by Portugal's anticlerical government in 1911.[13] It was not until three decades later that the Vatican and Portugal negotiated an agreement that bound the Church and state together.

The Concordat and Missionary Agreement was negotiated with Portugal in 1940. The agreement provided for close ties between Portugal and the Roman Catholic Church in the Portuguese colonies of Angola, Mozambique, and Guinea-Bissau. The Church was to conform to government policy in return for privileges and salaries for its clergy. This arrangement undermined the ability of the church to condemn Portuguese atrocities against Africans during the Frelimo liberation war. The aims of the church do not always coincide with those of the state.

The Protestant missionaries' presence in Mozambique dates to the nineteenth century. The travels of Scottish missionary David Livingstone in the Zambezi valley in the mid-nineteenth century led to the establishment of Universities Mission to Central Africa (UMCA) stations in Mozambique. Also establishing a presence in the last half of the nineteenth century was a Swiss congregation, the Free Evangelical Church of the Canton of Vaud in Switzerland, which penetrated Mozambique from South Africa and in 1872 first established a mission station at Spelonken in northern Transvaal among the Tsonga.

Most of the Tsonga people lived in their original home on the Mozambican coast. The first missionaries sent by the Free Evangelical Church to the Tsonga of Mozambique in 1882 were African converts. What is significant about the Free Evangelical Church is that Africans were at the forefront of spreading the gospel among their own people. African converts were instrumental in the establishment of mission stations. The stations witnessed tremendous growth within a relatively short period of time. By the mid-1880s, the Christianity spearheaded by the African ministers in Tsonga had an African flavor. Besides the conversions, ecstatic services that included participants being seized by the spirit were not uncommon. Adrian Hastings has aptly described this growth and expansion of the Free Evangelical Church among the Tsonga of Mozambique as "instant African Christianity," with its center at Rikatla.[14]

Converts acquired literacy skills and read the only available book *(buku)*, printed in Tsonga that contained extracts from scripture and a collection of hymns.[15] They were not content with what was contained in the buku and so began to embrace and incorporate ideas from African religions pertaining to evil spirits. Among the church faithful were three women converts: Lois, Ruti, and Mareta.[16] The last two were believed to have the power to drive out evil spirits. Also, polygyny and dowry were widely practiced by some of the converts at Rikatla without the approval of Spelonken, the mission headquarters in northern Transvaal. In a nutshell, the converts sought to give meaning to Christianity by combining their cultural and religious practices with the new faith. They saw no contradiction and thus believed that the two religious traditions, African and Christianity, could coexist and complement one another.

The first missionaries of the Methodist Episcopal Church went to Mozambique in 1890. Their pioneer missionary was Erwin Richards, who established a mission station at Chicuque. The evangelization process resulted in not only winning converts, but also in establishing institutions of learning. In 1905 Tezoura Navasse Mawoze became the first Mozambican to be ordained into the Methodist ministry. In 1963 Escrivao Anglaze Zunguze was elected the first indigenous Methodist bishop. The establishment of schools by the Methodist church opened opportunities for the faithful who wanted to pursue education. In this way, the church was equally instrumental in producing some of the first elite that would spearhead the struggle for independence.

ISLAM

Islam predates Christianity in Mozambique by several centuries. It reached Mozambique mainly as a result of the trade between Arabs and Mozambican coastal and hinterland communities.[17] As this trade across the Indian Ocean intensified, Arabs settlements began to dot the Mozambican coast north of Cape Delgado. From the various ports, Arab merchants traveled to the interior and established links with African chieftains. The latter obtained goods such as porcelain vases and bowls from China, rice and spices from Indonesia, and silks from India. In return, Africans exported gold and ivory. Islam grew out of these commercial relations because Arabs established mosques not only at the coast, but also in some hinterland trading posts where they conducted trade with the African chieftains.[18] African converts to Islam grew among the northern coastal communities, the Yao and the Swahili.

By the fifteenth century, when the first Portuguese reached Mozambique, Islam was already well established at the coast. When Vasco Da Gama and his crew reached Mozambique in 1498, they noted that the country was divided into two parts: the black African tribes of the hinterland and the Arab and Swahili traders who inhabited the central and northern coasts. The latter two groups were affluent and practiced the Islamic faith.

Despite winning converts in the central and northern parts of the country, Islam did not become a communal religion. It was accepted by small communities that found it appealing due to a number of reasons ranging from religion to economics. Conversion was via person-to-person contact. Since Arabs dominated the economic life in the coastal communities where they settled, conversion to Islam brought certain advantages such as power, access to the economic elite, literacy, and participation in the long-distance trade. Furthermore, Islam was culturally less disruptive because practices such as polygyny and the belief in a supreme deity and in the power of dreams and charms were not disallowed. Unlike Christianity, which called for complete abandonment of traditional practices such as polygyny that were incompatible with the new faith, Islam was accommodating, especially about some of the African cultural practices. African religious notions concerning ancestors, spirit possession, and witchcraft that are part of Swahili beliefs coexisted everywhere in Islam.

The introduction and presence of Islam in Mozambique did not entail war and mass conversion by the sword as in certain parts of Africa. It was by and large introduced through trade and peaceful interaction between Arabs and local communities. In spite of occasional tensions between Islam and the Portuguese colonial state, the religion has coexisted with traditional religions as well as Christianity in Mozambique without any major conflicts. This is in spite of the fact that during the late nineteenth century and the opening decades of the twentieth century the Portuguese were worried about the success of Muslim proselytization at a time when Roman Catholicism was faltering in gaining converts.[19]

Islam was in many ways a force for change because it is not only a religion, but also a way of life. It had a legal as well as an educational system. It had its holy book, the Quran, which had to be read and recited because it exposed students to various aspects of Islamic way of life: history, law, politics, commerce, architecture, and social practices. This called for literacy skills, which were taught in the few schools established among the Islamic communities, to enable students to read and understand the Quran, since at the lowest level they are expected to memorize the first 10 chapters of the holy book. At the very beginning of the twentieth century, there were 15 mosques and 10 Quran schools in the region of Angoche. Most of the converts in the region are reported to have known how to write their language in Arabic letters.

Muslim sects are not monolithic. They belong to different strands and brotherhoods. The two major *Sufi* orders, *tariqas,* emerged in Mozambique in the early twentieth century. The Shadhiliyya and the Qadiriyya were implanted at Mozambique Island, which became the point of expansion to adjacent territories and communities.[20] Since the Qadiriyya members are expected to read and engage in spiritual matters, Mozambique Island was at the very center of the Islamic intellectual revival that characterized the eastern coast of Africa during the early part of the twentieth century. The center produced many Islamic scholars who were instrumental in spreading the Qadiriyya strand into Malawi, Zanzibar, and the Comoro Islands. In return, Mozambique Island received many Islamic scholars.

Converts to Islam became monotheistic and held to five pillars of the faith: submission to the will of Allah (God) and acknowledgement of the Prophet Muhammad as his messenger; prayer five times a day facing Mecca; almsgiving to the poor and needy; fasting during the holy month of Ramadan; and pilgrimage to the holy city of Mecca at least once in a lifetime if one is able to. For the converts, adherence to these pillars called for the embrace of new spiritual values and strict moral principles.

A convert was accepted and became a member of the Islamic faith and community. As a result, intermarriage among Arabs and locals was not uncommon. Also, the impact of Arabs on the local communities is evident in the local languages, especially among the coastal communities where some Arabic words have found their way into the local dialects, and vice versa. In fact, spoken Swahili is an artful blend of Arab and Bantu elements, with a vocabulary drawn in almost equal proportions from each language. Islam also created local, regional, and international opportunities for the converts. It broadened their worldview and enabled them to interact with groups from various ethnic and racial backgrounds whose only common denominator was unity in the Islamic faith.

There were also aspects of Islam that did not sit well with African traditional practices, especially with respect to kinship and inheritance. Islam is a strongly patrilineal social order, which is in contrast to the matrilineal order that prevailed among some communities in Mozambique, such as the Yao.[21] It is interesting to note that the Yao maintained their social institutions. Retaining their customary law as well as matrilineal descent while embracing Islamic faith shows that a foreign religion cannot dismantle the established cultural practices that define a society. There always exists cultural dialogue during which two meeting cultures or ways of life compromise for the good of both traditions.

In contemporary Mozambique, Islam continues to coexist with the other faiths of Christianity and African traditional religion. The country has been spared the tensions that have gripped some African countries following the resurgence of Islamic fundamentalism demanding establishment of a theocracy or Islamic law as the basis of judicial system. Moslems in Mozambique are few and are overwhelmingly outnumbered by Christians and followers of African traditional religion. The country has also evolved and developed as a secular state. In the period immediately after independence, the Marxist-leaning Frelimo was intolerant of religion in public life and strove to build a strictly secular state, a development that has minimized the influence of religion on politics.

RELIGION, EDUCATION, AND DEVELOPMENT

The history of education in Mozambique is closely tied to the evolution and development of various religions in the country. Education was an integral part of traditional African religions. African traditional education served the process of cultural transmission and intergenerational communication. By

emphasizing culture and intergenerational communication, traditional education aimed at the preservation of the values and traditions of a society from
one generation to the next. It served to ensure respect for the age and gender
of each member of the society so that children came of age with full realiza-
tion of the proper roles of each generation and gender in society. It helped
to safeguard against breakdown in intergenerational communication and the
emergence of rebellious youth. A unique feature of traditional education is
that it was not only acquired, but also lived. Participation in sociopolitical and
religious institutions constituted some of the ways through which children
acquired education. In this regard, norms, mores, and folkways were widely
used to produce common understandings among members of a community
in order to enhance cultural growth and stability. Oral literature encompass-
ing fables, myths, and legends as well as proverbs was used to inculcate the
virtues of honor, respect, valor, value identification, and loyalty. Initiation
ceremonies, which are the subject of discussion in chapter 7, signified societal
commitment to the upbringing of children and their molding into responsible
citizens who put the interest of the society first.

Traditional education also imparted skills that enabled youths to build
on the prevailing conditions and catapult their society to a higher level
of development. Craftsmen and artists had to be apprenticed. Aspiring
medicinal practitioners had to learn the details of herbal medicine and serve
as an intern under the guidance of a renowned traditional healer. Traditional education among Mozambican communities was multifaceted and
emphasized both critical skills and moral values. The content of what was
imparted was determined by the society. The introduction of Islam as well
as Christianity impacted the way traditional education was imparted, but
failed to supplant it.

Arab settlements in the northern coastal part as well as pockets of settlements
in the central parts of Mozambique not only saw the emergence of mosques,
but also the establishment of Islamic education. Converts were taught reading
and writing as well as Arabic, a foreign language. Knowledge of Arabic was
and still is a necessity for a devout Muslim to read and understand the Quran.
They had to go to school at specific times and on a regular basis. As opposed
to traditional education, Islamic education was quite formal. The instructor
tested the pupils, and upon graduation they became part of the elite. The
values that were espoused were based on the Quran. However, Islamic education did not provide opportunities for higher education. It confined converts
to basic literacy skills. Only a select few were able to attain the elite status
that distinguished them from the rest of the converts. Also, it was not open
to those who did not embrace the Islamic faith. The overall impact of Islamic
education on Mozambicans was fairly limited and confined to its faithful.

Christianity has heavily impacted the development of education. By the mid-nineteenth century, Mozambique was home to many Christian churches, including Roman Catholics as well as non-Roman Catholic communities such as the Swiss Presbyterian Church, the Episcopal Methodist and Free Methodist Churches from the United States, the Anglicans, the Scandinavian Baptists, the International Holiness Mission, the South Africa General Mission, the Seventh Day Adventists, and the Pentecostal Assemblies of God. These churches established and ran elementary schools, albeit under the suspicious eye of a Portuguese colonial administration that distrusted Protestant missionaries.

However, neither the missionaries nor the Christian churches paid sufficient attention to the development of higher education. Even at the elementary level, schools were relatively few vis-à-vis the number of Africans. Most Mozambican students who wanted to pursue higher education either went to the neighboring South Africa or abroad to Europe or the United States. Nothing illustrates the inadequate educational opportunities in Mozambique more clearly than the fact that at independence 90 percent of the people of Mozambique could neither read nor write and only 5,000 had more than four years of elementary education. It is obvious that the Portuguese distrust of the missionaries restricted their ability to develop higher education. Similarly, the government did not want to produce an elite that would challenge the oppressive colonial system. It is not surprising that the first university in Mozambique was opened in 1962 in Maputo, but with only a few students. The missionary legacy lies in the fact that they were instrumental in nurturing Western education, which has emerged as the mainstream educational system for all Mozambicans. Also, the African nationalists went to mission schools. It was the Presbyterian Church that helped Eduardo Mondlane, the founding father of Mozambican Frelimo, with his elementary school in Mozambique, his secondary education in Transvaal, and his university education in South Africa and later in the United States.[22]

Besides education, the Christian churches have been involved in several projects that range from provision of healthcare facilities to development of water projects. The Catholic Church is the sponsor of many hospitals, clinics, as well as HIV/AIDS prevention programs in all its dioceses. Similarly, the United Methodist Church of Mozambique, under the leadership of Bishop Joao Machado, oversees the management of several schools, a hospital, clinics, and a trauma and conflict resolution center. The center plays an instrumental role in providing counseling services to victims of civil war as well as promoting reconciliation among the citizenry.

The local Christian churches usually enter into agreements with sister churches in the West in order to meet some of the development challenges.

It is against this backdrop that the UMC of Mozambique has a covenant with the Missouri Conference of the UMC in the United States. The Mozambique Initiative, which coordinates common matters of interest between the two provinces, has focused on development projects aimed at tackling poverty. The partnership has resulted in the construction of wells, which provide safe and clean drinking water to reduce waterborne diseases, thereby saving lives.

In sum, religion in contemporary Mozambique ministers to the individual by providing not only spiritual needs, but also material requirements. In times of stress and crises such as floods, drought, and famine, various Christian churches work closely not only with the government, but also with international agencies to deliver relief food and services to the citizenry.

NOTES

1. John S. Mbiti, *Concepts of God in Africa* (New York: Praeger Publishers, 1970), 141–143.

2. Harold Scheub, *The African Storyteller: Stories from African Oral Traditions* (Dubuque, IA: Kendall/Hunt Publishing Company, 1990), 165.

3. John S. Mbiti, *Prayers in African Religion* (Maryknoll, New York: Orbis Books, 1975), 32.

4. Mbiti, *Prayers,* 71.

5. Mbiti, *Prayers,* 80.

6. Mbiti, *Prayers,* 81.

7. Mbiti, *Concepts of God,* 172, 271.

8. Benght Sundkler and Christopher Steed, *A History of the Christian Church in Africa* (Cambridge: Cambridge University Press, 2000), 70.

9. Philip Curtin, et al., *African History: From Earliest Times to Independence* (London and New York: Longman, 1995), 253.

10. Sundkler and Steed, *A History,* 68.

11. Julius O. Adekunle, "East African States," in Toyin Falola, ed., *Africa Volume I: African History Before 1885* (Durham, NC: Carolina Academic Press, 2000), 197.

12. Adrian Hastings, *The Church in Africa, 1450–1950* (Oxford: Clarendon Press, 1994), 123.

13. Hastings, *The Church,* 564; William V. Bangert, S. J., *A History of the Society of Jesus* (St. Louis, MO: Institute of Jesuit Sources, 1986), 371, 401.

14. Bangert, *A History,* 443.

15. Bangert, *A History,* 442.

16. Bangert, *A History.*

17. Adekunle, "East African States," 196–200.

18. Adekunle, "East African States," 200–204.

19. Edward A. Alpers, "East Central Africa," in Nehemia Levtzion and Randall L. Pouwels, eds., *The History of Islam in Africa* (Athens: Ohio University Press, 2000), 309.

20. Alpers, "East Central Africa," 309–312.

21. Alpers, "East Central Africa."

22. Sundkler and Steed, *A History of the Christian Church,* 985.

3

Literature and the Media

INDIGENOUS LITERATURE

MOZAMBICAN SOCIETIES AND CULTURES developed creative literature long before the advent of Portuguese or Islamic literary traditions. While these traditions as introduced to Mozambicans at various times were largely defined and characterized by written language, Mozambican ethnic groups used oral literature as a means of communicating as well as retaining information about the past and present aspects of life. It is through oral literature, which constitutes an integral part of oral traditions, that most communities were able to pass their customs and traditions on from one generation to the next.[1] In subsequent years, following the onset of literacy, the Mozambican traditions were reduced to writing, making them readily available in various forms such as ethnographic works, creative writings, and current forms of media such as videos and audiocassettes. Oral literature was, and still is, an important aspect of literary tradition in Mozambique.

Oral literature proceeds on the premise that knowledge and expertise is in the minds of the members of the community, especially the elders. The genres of oral artistic expression include proverbs, songs, poetry, drama, plays, festivals, and oral narratives. This means that among Mozambican communities oral literature was the most important store of information. Face-to-face interaction was the primary form of communication as well as knowledge delivery. All aspects of life pertaining to what was acceptable or unacceptable were expressed directly by warning the individual and, perhaps more effectively, through verbal expressions such as story telling, idioms, songs, and dirges. Similarly, such expressions functioned to express the state of society as it was in the past and is in the present, and provided lessons for the future. Small wonder then that practically all communities in the country are rich in oral literature.

The telling of stories serves to inculcate certain desired values in young people. In rural areas where people live in nucleated villages and exhibit a strong sense of family and community, grandparents narrate stories about the family and community to their grandchildren. The stories are meant to emphasize certain virtues, a sense of unity and collective identity, relations between sexes, individual responsibility and accountability, honesty, courage, and hard work. Thus story telling went beyond mere entertainment. The intensity and complexity of the stories and accompanying songs had a tailored message that was suited to the needs of the listeners and embodied the common themes of shared heritage and communal welfare.

Some of the oral literature was performed during festivals that celebrated important events in the life of the individual or community: harvest, victory in war, birth, initiation, marriage, and death. Expressions evident in performances during such events show how ordinary artists and craftsmen produced literature and kept alive the societal way of life. This genre of oral literature is best exemplified by masquerade, which is a performance given by masked characters. This genre was widespread across the ethnic divide in Mozambique, especially in the various dances or songs in which the performers were masked to hide their identities.

Precolonial oral literature has not been given its due recognition because of the erroneous notion that it was not written down and therefore its authenticity is subject to doubt. Nothing could be further from the truth. Traditional precolonial education in Mozambique, as indeed in most African communities, was largely based on oral tradition. Oral literature was a big part of it. Indeed, it is not surprising that most Mozambican literary scholars have endeavored to give oral literature significant space in their writings in tandem with the new initiatives in poetry, theater, and the novel. Oral literature still exhibits continuing vitality and relevance in modern literary scholarship in Mozambique.

DRAMA

Missionaries introduced Portuguese literature to Mozambique. Religion played a big part in the way initial Portuguese drama/theater was presented to the Mozambicans. Roman Catholicism was the denomination most identified with the Portuguese. The Church was conservative and had no place for Mozambican customs and practices. Their primary purpose was to spread the faith in the country. Roman Catholicism was imposed on Mozambicans in order to supplant their faith and culture. Little regard was given to the pre-existing religion and culture, which were simply dismissed as less developed and sophisticated than the new faith and its attendant practices. As a result, Mozambican customs and practices were reduced to symbols of barbarism and evil. Plays, which were invariably religious in content, manifested the existing prejudice, as Africans were reserved roles for characters such as Judas and Lucifer, while the Portuguese acted the roles of angels and saints. The African was not only stereotyped, but was seen through the prism of the bad and the negative.

In the first half of the twentieth century, vaudeville was the most popular form of entertainment. By and large, these shows were meant for the Portuguese audience in Mozambique. Nevertheless, what is most important about vaudeville is its literary flowering in Mozambique during the first two decades of the twentieth century. This genre is best exemplified by works such as *Crime anica, Madalena, As aventturas de um heroi (Adventures of a hero)* and *Sua Alteza O Criador (His Highness the Creator)* by Carlos da Silva.[2] This tradition continued well into the 1930s and 1940s with publications by Fernando Baldaque and Arnado Silva, *Ponta Vermeil (Red Point,* 1931), Alexandre Cabral Campos, *A palhota de Mozambique (The Thatched Hut of Mozambique,* 1937), and *Zona perigosa (Danger Zone,* 1941). These productions elaborated and enhanced the idea of a benevolent colonial state and Portuguese colonialism and perpetuated the myth of the unsophisticated "native." The vaudeville was primarily state friendly, did not challenge the status quo, and thrived on the readily available audience of the settler population.

Written plays depicting the reality of Portuguese colonialism through the prism of the colonized Mozambicans were rather slow to develop because of the censorship that was put in place by the Portuguese colonial state. In essence, an objective interrogation of the colonial system was unacceptable because it meant questioning human values under colonial dictatorship. The few attempts to give voice to the Mozambican narrative from the colonized standpoint came through in Alfonso Ribeiro's *Tres setas apontadas para o futuro (Three Arrows Pointing to the Future,* 1959) and Lindo Lhongo's *Os dramatica sobre o lobolo (The Engagement* or *The Dramatic Discourse about the Purchasing of a Bride,* 1971). These two works are significant in the way they confronted the colonial plots that uncritically commented on colonial values. Ribeiro's play addressed the conflicts existent in the philosophies of human values as represented by the colonial present and the future devoid of colonial presence when universal human values will be seen for what they really are and not through the various prisms of race and one's position in the colonial order. Lhongo focused on objectivity and interrogation of the present-mindedness that was existent in Portuguese colonial narratives by reevaluating and renewing African culture and restoring it to its rightful place in Mozambican society. These two themes were echoed in other plays that appeared in the period immediately before independence: Lindo Lhongo's *As trinta mulheres de Muzelini (The Thirty Wives of Muzelini)*, Antonio Franciso's *Filhos da noite (Children of the Night)*, and Joao Fumane's *O feitico e a religiao (Sorcery and Religion)*.

While in the colonial period there was the political use of censorship in terms of plays that were produced and performed, the use of plays for political purposes did not cease after independence. Instead, the Frelimo government saw plays and attendant performances as powerful instruments that could be used effectively by the government to promote national healing and reconciliation. In this regard, plays produced after 1975 were not devoid of censorship because they were manipulated to further the government's agenda of building a one-party socialist state. It is against this backdrop that postcolonial plays in the country are largely defined. Plays by Orlando Mendes are some of the best that exemplify this genre: *Umminuto de silencio (One Minute of Silence)* and *Na Machamb de Maria—sabado as tres da tarde (On Maria's Small Farm—Saturday Afternoon at Three O'clock)*. These plays produced in 1975, the year of Mozambican independence, signified changed times from the preceding colonial period. It is important to note that the plays were hardly critical of the ideological path of the one-party socialist state because the Frelimo government was simply not receptive to criticism of its policies.

POETRY

Literary writing in Mozambique is largely a product of the interaction between indigenous societies and Portuguese colonialism. As a result, Mozambican literary scholars draw heavily on a strong oral tradition when communicating the experiences of Mozambican societies against the backdrop of Portuguese colonialism. Virtually all the poets in Mozambique use Portuguese. The local languages as well as oral traditions are usually infused as an important part of the poet's overall experience. The overriding theme is the suffering of the anonymous masses burdened by Portuguese dictatorship during colonial governance. The poets express the ravaging effects of hard labor and violence during colonialism, the desire for liberty, and the need to be united in the fight for liberation.

Jorge Rebello[3] best exemplifies this theme of colonial violence and the armed struggle for independence in his poems published in the anthology, *When Bullets Begin to Flower*. His poems such as "Poem for a Militant" and "Poem" demonstrate his commentary on colonial violence. In the former, Rebello speaks of the colonial chains that bound Mozambicans during

Portuguese dictatorship as well as the accompanying violence. But Rebello sees the solution in what he calls an iron rifle, which will in due course, "break the chains, open the prisons, kill the tyrants, and win back the land."[4] A sense of hope and optimism is thus evident because the iron rifle will bring freedom and justice. In the latter poem Rebello highlights colonial violence, "come, brother, and tell me your life; come, show me the marks of revolt which the enemy left on your body."[5]

Jose Craveirinha was until his death in 2003 one of the leading poets and literary scholars in the world of Lusophone literature. Writing in Portuguese, his many works of poetry include *Chigubo* (1964), *Cantico a um dio de Catrane* (1966), *Karingana ua Karingana* (1974), *Cela* (1981), *Maria* (1988), and *Hamina e Outros Contos* (1997). His 1974 collection of poetry, *Karingana ua Karingana,* is considered one of Africa's 100 best-selling books. His poems focus primarily on racism and Portuguese colonial domination. Among his many numerous accolades is the coveted Premio Camoes Award, the world's highest honor for Lusophone literature, which he won in 1991. His outstanding literary scholarship caused him to be considered several times for the Nobel Prize for Literature.

Poetry encompasses all aspects of life. Thus poetry in Mozambique is not just about colonial violence, armed struggle, liberation, and statehood. Love is an important and fundamental sentiment that is found in all human beings. Okpewho has eloquently noted that love poems are many and varied, dealing with sexual love, family love, and nationalistic love.[6] The Chopi poem "Nyagumbe! Nyagumbe!" is a sexual love poem about a bride engaging in a dialogue on her love for the bridegroom.[7] While Valente Malangatana's poem, "To the Anxious Mother," is also a love poem, it is focused on the appreciation of motherhood.[8] Thus while the two poems are about love, they represent different genres of love poetry.

Lack of education and other disadvantages have led to the underrepresentation of women in the literary field. However, one of the few names that stand out in the literary realm is Noemia de Sousa. She began writing her first poems in the late 1940s. Some of her most important poems include "Appeal" and "If You Want to Know Me."[9] She focuses on the subject of African women and their work. Her powerful poetic work has influenced a whole generation of women poets.

NOVELS

Postcolonial Mozambican fiction largely focuses on colonialism as well as the depth of trauma associated with colonial oppression and wars. Most of the novelists lived through the Portuguese colonialism and suffered due to the adverse colonial policies and abuse of human rights. The works of most of these novelists are a living testimony and commentary not only on their personal experiences, but also on the history of their country. Mia Couto's works best exemplifies the short-story writers whose themes echo this troubled history of Mozambique. Some of his most-read stories include "Voices Made Night" (1990) and "Every Man Is a Race" (1994) and are unique in the way they juxtapose narrative motifs and folk magic from the oral traditions with developments that depict the realities of war as they influence postcolonial Mozambique. One of the important attributes of his works is the way he goes beyond the colonial era to critique postcolonial Mozambique by highlighting the yawning gap between the elite and the masses. This is in spite of his loyalty to the ruling party, Frelimo. This may be attributed to his disillusionment with the government because postcolonial Mozambique has been bedeviled by violence and poverty, both of which were unimaginable when the masses were fighting the Portuguese to usher in peace and prosperity. His critique of the dictatorial tendencies of the Frelimo government, especially in the first years of independence, cannot be faulted.

Lina Magaia is another Mozambican short-story writer whose involvement in the Mozambican liberation war reveals the atrocities of the war not only in the decolonization era, but also in the immediate period of independence during the civil war that engulfed the country. One of her most widely read works is *Dumba Nengue: Run for Your Life.*[10] The words in the title, *Dumba Nengue,* a southern Mozambican proverb, literally translate as "Run for your life" or "You have to trust your feet." The words speak to the reality that confronted the people of southern Mozambique during the civil war in which the Renamo insurgency led to the deaths of thousands, the displacement of many more, and the destruction of the economy of a hitherto fairly prosperous region of the country. Magaia wove this powerful narrative from a wide array of interviews with victims who survived the civil war. Of significance is the 1987 massacre of 380 people in Dumba Nengue in southern Mozambique. The narrative is a testimony of the agony and political turmoil that defined Mozambique in the immediate period after independence. Her other titles, such as *Their Heads Were Crushed like Peanuts* and *Pieces of Human Flesh Fell on Belinda's Yard,* reveal the trauma and pain of independence. The sensational titles are emblematic of Magaia's novels that tell it as it is: the human rights abuses, the cheapness of human life, and the short, nasty, and insecure lives that Mozambicans had to endure. It is this sense of history that makes Magaia's narratives resonate with those who have closely followed not only the history of Lusophone Africa, but also other African countries that have had to go through the painful transition from colonialism to independence.

The themes of pain, suffering, sabotage, and insurgency also underpin the writings of Lilia Momple, a short-story writer whose novels capture not only the turbulent politics that have characterized Mozambique, but also the social cost to the family of having endured the incessant kidnappings and killings in the country during the civil war. Her literary publications include *No One Killed Suhura* (1988), *Neighbors—The Story of Murder* (1997), *The Eyes of the Green Cobra* (1997), and the short story, "Celina's Banquet," which was short-listed for the prestigious Caine Prize in 2001. Momple not only lived through the Portuguese colonialism, but she also participated in the liberation of her country by joining the Frelimo movement. In her novel, *Neighbors,* Momple weaves together present events and past memories and presents the contexts of Mozambican postcolonial dilemmas. She shows how the destabilization of Mozambique by the apartheid South African regime affected not only those who were involved in politics, but the ordinary citizenry as well. A denominator that characterizes her work is the deep sense of the Mozambican colonial past, the socialist experiment, and the deficit of democracy during the civil war period.

However, the novelist Lidia Jorge examines the colonial past with a focus on reconciliation. Her 1988 novel, *A Costa dos Murmurios (The Murmuring Coast),* is about how the colonizer and colonized interacted. The novel narrows the differences brought on by colonialism and its attendant negative attributes. It also points to the need for reconciliation by being sensitive to the colonial suffering to which Africans were subjected while at the same time focusing on how that colonial past traumatized the colonizers who were focused on maintaining the status quo. Both groups were badly bruised by the colonial experience, albeit Africans disproportionately, and hence the need to heal the wounds of the past by examining the common future that is neither vindictive nor dismissive of the reality that characterized colonialism.

NEWSPAPERS AND MAGAZINES

The major news agency in Mozambique is the Mozambique News Agency. It provides news in both Portuguese and English. There are also numerous newspapers and magazines, which cover information on local and international issues, politics, sports, people, and business. In this regard, the major newspapers and magazines cover commentaries on contemporary events as well as offer information on the current entertainment activities ranging from movies being shown to cultural entertainment in various theaters. From the newspapers and magazines one can also glean the latest information on real property, whether for investment or for rental purposes, as well as on banking and finance.

While most of the newspapers and magazines are printed, the development of the Internet has led to the rise of online newspapers and magazines as well. There are some that provide both print and electronic versions. The major newspapers and magazines are in Portuguese. *Noticias,* the major daily newspaper, has a circulation of slightly below 50,000, which is rather low taking into account the population of the country. The other major daily is *Diario do Mozambique,* whose circulation averages less than 25,000. These two major daily newspapers are largely representative of the ruling party. Even the weekly publication, *Domingo,* is representative of the ruling party. Its circulation averages less than 30,000. As a result of the looming influence from the ruling party these major publications expound on party policies, albeit not always critically. They sell more than the privately owned newspapers because public offices get copies.

The role of the government in the newspapers is not surprising taking into account the history of the country. During the colonial period, the Portuguese colonial state did not allow media pluralism to prevail in the country. It controlled the media and the flow of information. This development hindered the rise of independent and free media in the country. After the attainment of independence the Frelimo government took the country on a socialist path by focusing on a one-party state, which by its nature is intolerant of alternative viewpoints outside of the party ideology. Media pluralism remained unacceptable. In fact, the media was patronized by the state and information manipulated in order to support the government's position on the pertinent issues of the day. It is this legacy that explains the government's enormous influence on the foregoing major publications as well as radio and television, which are discussed in the next section.

One year before the cessation of hostilities due to the civil war, the government of Mozambique passed the first new democratic media law in 1991. The law was supposed to widen the democratic space and encourage pluralism of the media. The result has been the growth in the number of newspapers, some of which are independently owned; among them, *Zambezi, Metical, Fim de Semena,* and *Canal de Mozambique* are some of the many smaller independent newspapers. The rise of independent newspapers has contributed to the widening of the democratic space and brought a sense of balance in the coverage and analysis of the news. The privately owned MediaCoop Group of Mozambique publishes the daily *Mediafax,* the weekly *Savana* magazine, and the English *Mozambique Inview,* a biweekly publication.

Metical, which was founded by the late investigative journalist Carlos Cardos, is another privately owned magazine. Cardos was a cofounder of MediaCoop in 1992 before leaving it to found and edit *Metical* in 1997. As an investigative journalist, Cardos exposed the country's drug-smuggling syndicates as well as fraud and embezzlement that involved prominent businessmen and politicians. His magazine also exposed the theft of millions of shillings from the then state-owned Commercial Bank of Mozambique. *Metical* exhibits high standards in journalism and exemplifies the good that can come from a free and independent press. It has to be noted that such expositions are usually unacceptable to those who are the beneficiaries of such drug syndicates, bank frauds, and thefts of public funds. Cardoso paid the ultimate price when he was killed in 2000 at the age of 48. Despite such setbacks, Mozambique has a vibrant press, and with the liberalized political and economic situation in the country, the number of newspapers, both in the mainstream media and alternative press, has witnessed marked growth since the 1991 media law.

Besides exposing the ills that bedevil society, newspapers and magazines, and indeed the entire media, have been instrumental in the campaign against HIV/AIDS. As a result, foreign assistance has been provided to Mozambican media to develop coverage aimed at counseling and advocacy for the prevention of HIV/AIDS in the communities. World Bank, USAID, NORAD, UNDP, and UNAIDS have all donated generously to the campaign against the pandemic. Part of the funding has also been used in the training of journalists. One of the major consequences has been the attempt to expand the constitutional right to information by funding newspapers and magazines in various ethnic languages and outside of Maputo, where there has been a heavy concentration of the media. In this way newspapers, magazines, billboards, radio, and television have all been mobilized to help fight against stigma and discrimination.

The use of the Internet is also gaining momentum, especially in the cities. In 2005 there were 7,228 Internet hosts and hundreds of thousands of users. This is generally a small proportion of the urban population. The Internet is increasingly becoming a popular medium of communication and accessing information by the educated in Maputo. Indeed, some newspapers and magazines in Mozambique can be accessed online. Some businesses too have web pages with vital information that can be accessed by potential clients. While the number of those relying on and accessing the Internet is still comparatively low, the emergence of Internet cafes in Maputo points to the not too distant future when the Internet will occupy an important place in the Mozambican media.

RADIO AND TELEVISION

The official government radio service in the country is Radio Mozambique. It broadcasts in Portuguese, English, Afrikaans, and local languages. Radio Mozambique is owned by the government and controls a disproportionately large share of the market. It has regional distribution that covers most of the country through a number of transmitters and stations located in each province. However, the liberalization of the media has resulted in the establishment of various radio stations that are independently owned such as Radio Encontro, Xai Xai, Radio Paz, and RDP Africa among many others.

The independently owned radio stations do offer a wide array of programs ranging from entertainment and sports to political and economic news analysis, but they have been unable to effectively challenge the dominance of the state-owned Radio Mozambique by eroding its disproportionate control of the market share. One of the reasons that account for the independently owned stations' inability to compete with Radio Mozambique is that they have a limited broadcasting range. Also, they invariably choose to be a local or community radio station, which leads to a much smaller audience because the local and regional languages are used and people that do not belong to that community cannot understand the broadcast. Furthermore, they are unable to compete with the government-owned station that is heavily subsidized through grants from the state.

The television network in Mozambique is less developed than radio broadcasting. Reception in most of the rural areas is not only poor, but nonexistent. TVM dominates the market. Other privately owned television networks include Television Miramar and RTP Africa, which has a large audience that is second only to TVM. RTP is the Portuguese public broadcaster and is open to viewers on an open channel. Other available networks include South African TV and Zimbabwe TV. The presence of numerous television networks is again largely due to the liberalized media market. This is good for Mozambican viewers because they have a choice of what to watch.

The major challenge that the media faces in Mozambique is how to strengthen distribution systems through the establishment of local centers of communication in order to ensure the access to and existence of pluralistic media across the entire country. Whether one is looking at print or electronic media, in the case of newspapers, the Internet, and radio and television, it is obvious that the vibrant media has a marked presence in Maputo and southern Mozambique. Yet the central and northern parts of the country are less well served by the pluralistic media.

NOTES

1. Jan Vansina, *Oral Tradition as History* (Madison: University of Wisconsin Press, 1985).

2. Martin Banham, Errol Hill, and George Woodyard, eds., *The Cambridge Guide to African and Caribbean Theatre* (Cambridge: Cambridge University Press, 1994), 13.

3. Jorge Rebello was born in 1940 in the capital city of Laurenco Marques, now Maputo. He is a lawyer and journalist and joined Frelimo during the liberation war. Rebello became the director of information for the movement during the liberation war. It is least surprising, therefore, that his poems focus on colonial violence and the struggle for independence.

4. Gerald Moore and Ulli Beier, eds., *The Penguin Book of Modern African Poetry* (New York and London: Penguin Books, 1998), 221.

5. Moore and Beier, *Modern African Poetry,* 220.

6. Isidore Okpewho, ed., *The Heritage of African Literature* (Essex, U.K.: Longman Group, 1985), 38.

7. Okpewho, *The Heritage,* 41–43.

8. Okpewho, *The Heritage,* 48.

9. Arlene A. Elder, "Who Can Take the Multitude and Lock the Cage?: Noemia de Sousa, Micere Mugo, Ellen Kuzwayo: The African Women's Voices of Resistance," *Matatu: Journal of African Culture and Society* 3, 6 (1989): 77–100.

10. Lina Magaia, *Dumba Nengue: Run for Your Life—Peasant Tales of Tragedy in Mozambique* (Trenton, NJ: Africa World Press, 1988).

4

Art and Architecture/Housing

MOZAMBIQUE IS RENOWNED for its richness in art, which is complex and diverse. Mozambican art is the pillar of its culture. It conveys political, economic, and social themes in a visual and powerful way. The art of most Mozambican societies mirrors the cultural richness and diversity of Mozambican society in its totality. Its art has not been immune from the various influences that have impacted society in the recent past. Thus, Mozambican art is not only real and alive, but it has also embraced those various external influences. These attributes also characterize architecture and housing in the country. There exist traditional architectural designs that depict African housing, exhibited by the typical homesteads that dot the rural countryside; European designs that are very much evident in the cities; and Islamic patterns epitomized by mosques and Arab settlements that are characteristic of Moslem enclaves in Mozambique.

This chapter examines art and architecture/housing in Mozambique by taking into account the foregoing rich heritage and diversity, especially the many and varied influences that have shaped its developmental stages in the recent past to produce what is existent in the country today. Various forms of art such as sculpture, painting, textiles, and fashion are analyzed. The chapter also delves into a consideration of the artists whose creativity is manifested in contemporary Mozambique. Finally, rural and urban settlements, especially types of housing and associated patterns, are examined against the backdrop of various cultural groups and their attendant spatial settings.

TRADITIONAL AFRICAN ART

Body Decoration

Body art was widely practiced in Mozambique well into the colonial period. Various communities embraced body art and decoration, and tattoos were widely used for beauty and elegance more or less similar to the way they are seen in the West. Body decoration and tattoos took various geometric forms. The more elaborate the decoration or tattoo the more the person captured the public eye. Women's decoration and tattoos were more elaborate than those of men. Among the Makonde, the community universally accepted the lip plug, called *ndona,* and its members wore it.[1] The making of the lip plug entailed boring a small hole in a person's upper lip with a needle or thorn. After the hole was made, a twig was inserted to widen it. This was continued as the person came of age, albeit with larger twigs, so that by the time the person reached puberty a small circular disk of ebony was inserted to plug the hole that existed in the upper lip. The lip plug was less common among men. Even among women, the practice is no longer as widespread as it was before the 1970s.

The making of such lip plugs, tattoos, or other similar body decorations was not painless. Stoner has given elaborate description of what the making of the lip plug entailed.[2] He asserts that it involved piercing or cutting the skin using sharp objects such as knives and/or blades. Charcoal ash was then rubbed to sterilize and clean the place that was cut or pierced. Upon healing, the dark spots remained. If thicker marks were required, the cut was supposed to be deeper, and this occasionally involved having to repeat the exercise many times.[3] To an external observer, such undertakings would raise many questions about why people underwent such pain to beautify themselves.

However, the way a generation or society defines beauty dictates the way its members act. Indeed, to be accepted by peers and society an individual had to adhere to societal demands. The Makonde, for example, also filed or chipped their teeth after initiation as a mark that they had gone through the ritual and attained full membership as adults in their community.[4] These were traditions handed down from one generation to the next—there was no exit strategy. Furthermore, individuals cherished those marks as a badge of identity and belonging to one's social or ethnic group.

With modern forces of social change such as education, missionary Christianity, and urbanization, scarification practices are becoming less elaborate than they were during the previous centuries. For example, lip plugging, filing or chipping of teeth, and elaborate decorations are dying out because they are seen as cruel and inhuman. Indeed, teenagers growing up in the cities are abandoning some of the practices. Also, the availability of modern surgical instruments has made tattooing less painful than it was in traditional society. Tattooing also does not carry the social and ritual weight that it once had in traditional society.

Masks

Masks are important in Mozambican society, and they serve a number of different functions. First, masks are used widely during initiation, memorial, and funerary occasions. The mask represents a personality, and as a result the wearer of a mask assumes the personality that the mask depicts. He imitates the person and is supposed to act in exactly the same way as the individual. As a result, if the imitated character is a spirit the mask will be made to reflect that spirit in such a way that the spirit is seen as real and alive. The mask is decorated and presented with all the features that characterize that spirit. If the representation is of a departed ancestor, the mask will be made to replicate the facial features of the person, albeit with some mystification because, having joined the spirit world, he had assumed a new identity. The masked figure comes back to life and is able to be seen by younger people who never witnessed the ancestor in real life.

Masks also serve as commentaries on the prevailing state of events in a clan, community, or the country. In a sense, makers of masks are supposed to be innovative and capture the spirit and mood of the occasion at a specific time in the history of the group. That innovation was quite evident during the era of Portuguese colonialism, when masks were used as political commentaries on the adverse impact of Portuguese colonial rule. Masks could be made to represent a white colonial police officer or administrator. In such cases, the masks were painted pink and the wearer of the mask ridiculed the colonial police officer or administrator by imitating how the official acted. In this way, they critiqued the colonial officials because their identity was concealed. Since it was anathema to unmask or reveal the identity of the wearer of the mask, the imitator was immune from arrest or punishment. At any rate, such performances were done before friendly audiences. Thus masks also served to depict reality in a way that society understands and interprets.

Masks also serve to make fun of or to ridicule a person, an institution, or a custom. By poking fun, a message is passed to the effect that certain behavior and/or custom is unwarranted. Since the ridicule is exhibited in a way that people laugh about it, the message is internalized, and positive reinforcement is accomplished without upsetting a person. In such cases, masks provide educational value that helps rid the society of undesired practices without unsettling the societal equilibrium by alienating some of its members.

Masks are also indispensable in various performances such as traditional music and dance. Most Mozambican societies have embraced masks as part and parcel of their costumes during performances pertaining to traditional dances during rituals. Masks and body painting add an aesthetic touch to the dance by making it appear authentic. It is important to note that this is still very much part of the Mozambican society. During school music festivals, it is not uncommon to see the soloist with a decorated body and wearing a mask to capture the true mood and spirit that informs the music and/or dance being performed. While some practices such as elaborate scarifications and lip plugging are currently frowned upon, masks and body decorations are making their way into mainstream modern life, especially in art and music curriculum.

Finally, masks can be utilized to reflect a desired mood that befits a desired state. Thus one can be made to look serious, funny, clownish, frightening, beautiful, or intriguing. It is these differing moods that make masks reflective of the occasion being performed, or relived. Indeed, it provides one with the opportunity to assume a mood and act it out for a few moments. The use of masks and body decoration cuts across all ethnic groups in Mozambique.

The making of masks is a laborious exercise that requires creativity. A wide array of local materials is often used in making masks, including wood, raffia, animal skins, bark cloth, and cowrie shells. In addition, other items such as natural paints and dyes are used for decoration. Beads, bottle tops, and an assortment of toys are also added as part of the decoration. While the decorated mask is admirable, it is the way the performer uses it that eventually thrills and captivates the audience. In a sense, the mask constitutes a means of pleasure and enjoyment that is best attained by the skillful performance of the acting character. The combination of mask and performance deepens vision and commentary by setting imagination free.

Sculpture

If there is any one form of art that stands in Mozambique, it is sculpture. Mozambican sculpture exhibits both features of realism as well as abstract forms. The community that is most well known for its sculpture is the Makonde.[5] Their woodcarvings are used to produce both themes of realism and abstract forms. Realism in Makonde art is quite evident in the way men and women are depicted smoking, fetching water, or engaging in other daily activities. In this regard there is sensitivity to gender roles. It is quite common to see women presented as mothers, pregnant, carrying children, or cooking. The impression one gets is the story of an overwhelmed woman who is shouldering the burden of motherhood.

Similarly, there are works that show the moods of the human characters: anger, joy, frustration, and conflict. One of the most interesting features associated with human character and challenges is the ability of the Makonde sculptor to create large sculptures of three to six feet with multiple characters joined together.[6] This is not surprising, because the human body is at the very center of this art. Yet the human body in the African context does not exist entirely on its own, because it is part and parcel of the wider lineage, clan, and ethnic group, and hence the emphasis on multiple characters that makes the whole body function well. Nkatunga, a renowned Makonde sculptor, has been one of those whose works depict this theme of "family tree," with pieces that are carved from single pieces of ebony wood.[7] Nkatunga has ably captured the daily life in a rural community that is still very much steeped in extended family relationships. This, however, does not mean that the artists are only concerned with the large sculptures, thereby having no place for small ones.

Besides real and naturalistic works, there is also the preoccupation with the abstract form. Representation of spirits is quite common. A sculptor is supposed to penetrate areas of the human consciousness that are part of man's deepest and oldest experiences, the spiritual dimension. Representation of spirits is a common theme in Mozambican art. Sculptors often stress the functions of their subjects by classifying spirits: fighting, fertility, good, and bad. These spirits are depicted in various shapes and sizes. Good ancestral spirits are sometimes in the form of figurines of female ancestors. These are miniature in size and can be used as amulets for protection. A departed ancestor can be made to be present and offer protection to individuals as they go about their daily activities. The evil ones exhibit an element of disability such as distorted faces or missing limbs.

Painting

Painting as an art form is very popular in Mozambique. Indeed, one of the most famous Mozambican artists is Malangatana.[8] His paintings are unique in the way they show the story of Mozambique from the colonial through the postcolonial era, depicting the rich history of the various political and developmental challenges Mozambique went through in its twentieth-century journey. The common themes are the struggles during the colonial period when he was growing up, liberation, and civil war. Malangatana's paintings are full of the lively figures that he has created and that have since been widely copied. What is most notable in Malangatana's paintings is the very able way in which he captures Mozambique's contemporary history.

Functional and Aesthetic Crafts

Mozambican communities, homesteads, households, and individuals exhibit various forms of functional and aesthetic crafts. People make various crafts for their daily use as well as for decorations. Use and aesthetic values are not inseparable; they are complementary. Pottery has been widely used by Mozambican communities from time immemorial. While the primary functions included cooking, drinking, and water storage, the more refined and elaborate the decoration was, the better. In cases where the items were to be sold, those that were decorated attracted attention and fetched higher prices. In this context, there is direct correlation between the item's use and decorative value and its price. Ornamented objects were highly cherished and valued.

In practicing agriculture, farm implements were locally produced by blacksmiths. In the absence of local production of such implements farmers imported them from communities that produced them. Even in such cases, blacksmiths tried to refine their products and ornament them so that the items could capture the buyer's attention and therefore sell. With the increased commercial relations between Mozambicans and the Portuguese, local hoes could not compete with the imported ploughs that were much more effective in tilling large chunks of land within a relatively short period of time. This began to undermine local blacksmiths. Mozambicans also produced baskets, mats, pestles for grinding meal, and handles for axes and hoes. All these tools had functional value, yet were produced by local artisans.

Various communities also worked with available materials such as wood, cane, sisal, and shells to make practical items. The desire to make ornamented items was always a factor, and items were decorated for pleasure. In this regard, tapestries made in the province of Zambesia and shell ornaments made on Mozambique Island in Nampula Province were some of the most admired crafts from Mozambique.

ARCHITECTURE—RURAL AND URBAN SETTLEMENTS

Rural Settlement and Traditional House Types

Most Mozambicans live in rural areas largely based on the kinship system—people who are related usually inhabit one region. Indeed, ethnic groups in Mozambique live in specific regions where they practice their customs and traditions. Homesteads dot the rural landscape. Each homestead comprises a number of households where various members of the family of the head of the homestead live. The head of the homestead is usually an elder, and the various households within his homestead provide an assurance that his family is thriving. This does not mean that he has absolute control over the various households within the homestead. Nothing could be further from the truth. Each household is to a large extent autonomous in the way food is sourced, processed, and distributed to the various people within that household. Nevertheless, when members of the same extended family live together in the homestead the sense of identity and sharing is enhanced. A homestead is therefore not only an architectural definition, but also a social arrangement. Thickets to protect the residents against raiders usually surrounded a homestead.

A typical Mozambican homestead has a predetermined set-up such that when you enter the home a casual look will make it obvious the house that belongs to the head of the homestead, his wives in terms of seniority, and the children. A homestead's pattern sends a specific message to a visitor versed in tradition and custom about whether the owner is a monogamist or practices polygyny, whether the individual has married children or not, and whether the person is regarded as an important person in the clan and community. The more the houses, the more members in the family and, therefore, the more power the owner wields in society. The elder of the home usually has a house within the center of the courtyard that is preserved for his guests for purpose of relaxation. Among the Makonde the house is known as *chitala*.[9] Elders receive guests and use the chitala for meeting and discussing important issues, away from the children and other frequent guests who are not supposed to be privy to that kind of confidential information. The use of the owner of the homestead's house also serves to bestow some privacy to the wives' houses so that they can prepare their food without interruptions from the visitors. It is also used as a dining place for the elder's visitors, and blacksmiths and carvers store their tools as well as musical instruments in the chitala. In a sense, the chitala is the focal point in the homestead from which the entire homestead is governed.

Mango trees usually shade the courtyard. The courtyard provides the children with space to play, and children from various houses and/or homesteads play together. The social interaction is deemed important because children learn to tolerate one another. It also enables social bonds. Children are cherished in African society because they represent the future of the community, continuity, and wealth and prosperity. They are seen as a blessing from God and ancestors. An African could be rich, but without children the riches are insignificant. The person is not esteemed by the society as the case would if the marital life were graced with children. Thus a homestead with many children playing in the courtyard is something any elder yearns for. Because of the open space, adults can easily monitor the movements and activities of the children to ensure that they are not hurt. Indeed, a typical house has two doors: One looks out on the courtyard while the other usually looks at the back of the house. The latter often lead to a small garden within the homestead where vegetables are grown.

The construction of houses in contemporary Mozambique is dependent on environment, economic status, taste, and customs. Environment will dictate the pattern as well as the sourcing of materials for use in construction. The availability of materials will depend on whether the region is well endowed with rainfall that supports dense vegetation. Such areas provide the inhabitants with the wood that is usually used to make poles to support thatched roofs. The houses are invariably circular in shape. In the hot and humid areas houses still retain the circular shape and conical shapes with a column in the middle of the house to support the ceiling. There are no internal walls/partitions, thereby leaving only one large room. Reeds, mud, or clay are widely used. Mud structures survive well in hot and humid areas. The mud also withstands heavy rainfall, especially when the sun dries it out after a heavy downpour. It is not uncommon to find the mud walls thickened, with spaces carved on the inside to serve as shelves. Also, the houses are well ventilated by leaving spaces between the wall and the roof through which air can enter the rooms. The wall and the floor are generally supposed to have a fine smooth finish and are decorated with carved designs. The intricate styles of decoration exhibit both traditional and contemporary scenes. The decoration can depict beads, pottery, or persons as well as cars, bicycles, and clocks. It is the role of the woman to beautify the house by carving these designs. It is acceptable and not uncommon for a person to copy the design styles. The various styles show a lot of innovation and creativity.

The construction of a house in traditional society was not a one-person affair. People sought help from members of the extended family in putting up the house. Members would volunteer their time and energy by digging holes, cutting grass or reeds, mixing mud/clay and transporting materials to the construction site at no pay. Helping one's own family member was the most significant factor. The person being helped was expected to provide food and drinks for the volunteers. The volunteers would also be helped when their turn came to construct a house. Even though the house belonged to the individual, the members of the extended family felt proud that one of their own had come of age. The house provided shelter for other members of the family besides the owner. The owner would be receiving extended relatives to share his food, drinks, and even shelter in cases of need.

However, the rural housing is undergoing change. Mozambicans have served as migrant workers to and from the cities, both within the country and in South Africa, for well over a century. Also, a number of citizens have acquired Western education and are very much active in the formal sector of the economy as professionals. As a result of these developments the embrace and transplanting of urban designs into the rural countryside, especially by those with economic resources to put up modern housing, is being seen in the construction of modern homes. They build houses made of brick and corrugated iron sheets. The pattern is also changing from circular to rectangular.

The houses are better ventilated because of the large windows as well as many and more spacious rooms that are atypical of traditional houses. Besides, these modern houses are generally freestanding housing units for one nuclear family as opposed to the traditional ones that exhibited an extended family social pattern.

URBAN SETTLEMENTS AND HOUSING

Urbanism in Mozambique predates Portuguese colonialism in the country. Indeed, the Portuguese found well-established city-states, the leading of which was Sofala.[10] The cities were mainly situated along the east coast of Mozambique. However, the cities were less densely populated than they are today. Housing was fairly adequate. The architecture reflected the demographic composition of the cities: Africans and Arabs. The arrival of the Portuguese and the subsequent development of the modern economy led to the rise of many and varied opportunities that revolved around city life. New cities emerged, while the old ones expanded into the adjacent rural countryside. Even though most Mozambicans still live in the rural countryside, more people are migrating to the cities. This is because urban areas, especially the larger ones, are seen as the focal points to go to in search of employment opportunities. As a result, the cities are unable to provide enough housing to cope with the surge in urban population.

Maputo, previously known as Lourenco Marques when it was the colonial capital, is the leading urban settlement and capital city of Mozambique.[11] The independent government of Mozambique renamed Lourenco Marques as Maputo, which is a traditional African name that means "home village." Maputo serves as the commercial hub of the country. Being a port, Maputo transacts import and export trade. Its industrial base consists of food-processing industries as well as the manufacturing industry. Tourism is also a major sector that brings revenue to the city.

The city of Maputo has gone through various developmental stages. The area where Maputo currently stands was first explored by in 1544 by Laurenco Marques, a Portuguese trader.[12] The city was named after Marques when it was founded as a permanent settlement in the late eighteenth century. However, the small settlement did not grow into a major trading center even after its founding, because the Portuguese focused their activities on the Mozambique island down to Sofala and the immediate hinterland along the Zambezi River. The area around Maputo was of little economic relevance to the Portuguese. It was not until the last decades of the nineteenth century that Maputo began to grow into a Portuguese colonial city. This growth was precipitated by developments in South Africa, especially the discovery of gold and diamonds in the area around Johannesburg in the 1870s and 1880s. Maputo was recognized as the capital of Mozambique in 1888.[13] Six years later a railroad linking the city to Transvaal mine fields in South Africa was completed. The development of rail and road infrastructure proceeded at a fast pace in response to the demands necessitated by the mineral revolution in South Africa. Maputo became a major export port for South African minerals. Furthermore, many Mozambicans went to the South African mines as migrant workers. The link between Mozambique and South Africa was firmly established, and Maputo became an important nodal point in the link.

Maputo became a model colonial city with a clear distinction between predominantly white residential areas and the shantytowns where Africans lived. The former was referred to as "cement city" and the latter as "canico" areas.[14] The import of the two categorizations is clear. The "cement city" signified the permanent and elaborate structures, which reflected the splendor and opulence that characterized that part of the city, while *canico* referred to the local reed that was used to construct the houses occupied by African workers. The canico areas were the shantytowns where people of low income who were invariably Africans lived. Colonial Maputo was two cities in one, largely divided along racial lines.

In sum, Maputo was planned and developed as a European city with wide boulevards, public gardens, and parks as well as paved sidewalks complete with mosaic tiles. It is an impressive city, with most of its public buildings marble-fronted. Interestingly enough, Maputo is one of the unique cities in Africa that embraced and combined African art in the making of colonial structures. The Portuguese architect Amancio d'Alpoim Guedes, who was inspired by traditional African art, added shapes and symbols from native architecture to his modern constructions.[15] Examples of this innovation are the long spines that protrude like poles from the outer corners of Guedes's buildings, chimneys shaped like mushrooms, and wall mosaics featuring African designs. This aesthetic and structural blend demonstrates the possibilities of African and Western art and architecture coexisting side by side in African cities.

Despite its planned development, Maputo, like many other African capitals, has been forced to contend with the influx of Africans into the cities. The result has been the expansion of shantytowns. Soon after independence, the socialist government of Mozambique embarked on the nationalization of private property, a development that saw many people move into the "cement city." This led to the deterioration of the condition of the houses as well as stress on the available amenities that were initially meant for a low population density zone. The decision was reversed after the government abandoned the socialist path and embraced a capitalist economy as well as respect for private property. Maputo thus has continued to see the growth of shantytowns, which are high population density areas, as more and more low-income people moved into the city. With a population of well over two million people, Maputo is unlikely to provide adequate decent housing for all of its population.

The second largest city in Mozambique is Beira. It is the capital of Sofala province and is important as a seaport that serves not only Mozambique but also the landlocked hinterland countries of Zimbabwe, Malawi, and Zambia. It also serves the Democratic Republic of Congo. The city has important rail links that extends to all the countries that it serves as a major seaport. Beira's history dates to the first millennium when it was founded as an old Muslim settlement on the Mozambique channel.[16] However, it did not grow into a major port until the late nineteenth century, during the peak of European colonization of Africa, and it became the headquarters of the Portuguese Mozambique Company in 1889. It got another lease on life in 1892 when the British South African Company, which was owned by Cecil Rhodes, began the construction of the railroad from Beira to Salisbury (Harare).[17] Besides the export sector that is the main backbone of the city's economy, Beira has a diverse economic base that boasts of fishing, food processing, manufacturing, and tourism. Its architecture is modern and Western in style, reflecting the influence of the Portuguese and the entrenched economic interests of various companies allied with the West. The city has modern restaurants, hotels, and sandy beaches that are often frequented by tourists. The irony is that domestic tourism is not well developed, and as a result very few Africans frequent the beaches as tourists. The tourism industry provides the locals with employment opportunities.

Another major city is Nampula, which was founded in the middle of the last century[18] and is located in the northeast of the country between Lake Malawi and the port of Nacala. The commercial railroad passes through the city, which was founded by the Portuguese in the late 1940s by draining a swamp. They subsequently built schools, stadiums, churches, offices, and houses with the hope of making it the metropolis of northern Mozambique. Today the city is a thriving commercial center with many banks, trading companies, and businesses that have relocated to the area. Nampula also serves the adjacent farming communities who ship their merchandise through the city.

The cities in Mozambique present a distinction in terms of those who have the means to afford and pay for better housing and those of low income who are barely surviving. Decent apartments and houses are available for those who have the money to pay for such apartments/homes. They usually have three or more bedrooms with all amenities such as water, electricity, telephone, and security. For those renting, some are self-contained, having a refrigerator, television, and high-quality furniture. Such decent housing is found in fairly secure areas that are less congested and well landscaped.

Urban housing for the affluent is well planned. Building codes are strictly adhered to. Houses are made of stone and/or brick. They can either be ranch or one/two stories in height. The more elaborate the house, the more the financial clout of the occupant. The homes are sometimes fenced and a servants' quarters provided for the maid, a colonial legacy that emphasized the distinction between the master and the house help. The urban elite who own such residences invariably employ two or three helpers to assist with domestic chores. They also cherish the idea of nuclear family as opposed to that of the extended family. In a sense, the affluent in those areas have by and large embraced the Western lifestyle. The elaborate homes are in low population density areas that were previously occupied by the Portuguese colonial administration officials and the business elite.

The designs of such homes speak to the multiracial heritage of Mozambique—African, Asian, and Portuguese. Along the coastal cities the long presence of the Arabs during the high point of dhow trade between the East African coast and the Arabian seaports is quite evident in the Islamic architecture as well as mosques. The areas previously dominated by the Portuguese elite attest to the opulence and grandeur, power struggles and animosity between the Portuguese and local inhabitants on the one hand and the Arabs on the other. A visit to Maputo, the city with the tower, is instructive of this past, which was characterized by tension and economic inequality.

The low-density, elaborate, and spacious homes that are found in the affluent areas are a sharp contrast to the high population density areas, which in some cases have seen the emergence of shantytowns. Major cities such as Maputo, Beira, Nampula, Tete, and Quelimane are all experiencing shortages in housing, especially for those of low income. Because of the lack of adequate housing, temporary homes in shantytowns have sprung in the last couple of decades. In the shantytowns, houses have minimal sanitation and sometimes a complete absence of electricity. The houses in the shantytowns are small and congested. Sharing a room is not uncommon. Those with two or more rooms usually accommodate relatives from the rural areas who come to town in search of jobs, leading to stress on available resources. Buildings in shantytowns are largely temporary, because most of them are not sanctioned by the state. The owners do not follow any building codes, and the buildings are vulnerable to adverse conditions, especially floods, fire outbreaks, and epidemics.

Notes

1. John Stoner, *Makonde* (New York: Rosen Publishing Group, 1998), 37–38.

2. Stoner, *Makonde*, 38–40.

3. R. S. James, *Places and Peoples of the World: Mozambique* (New York and Philadelphia: Chelsea House Publishers, 1988), 69–70.

4. Stoner, *Makonde,* 40.

5. Sidney Littlefied Kasfir, *Contemporary African Art* (London: Thames and Hudson, 1999), 109–112.

6. Jason Laure and Ettagale Blauer, *Enchantment of the World: Mozambique* (Chicago: Childrens Press, 1995), 70–71.

7. Laure and Blauer, *Enchantment,* 71.

8. James, *Mozambique,* 73; Laure and Blauer, *Enchantement,* 70.

9. Stoner, *Makonde,* 22.

10. Malyn Newitt, *A History of Mozambique* (Bloomington and Indianapolis: Indiana University Press, 1995), 3–8.

11. Barry Munslow, "Maputo," in Kevin Shillington, ed., *The Encyclopedia of African History, Volume II* (New York and London: Fitzroy Dearborn, 2005), 943-944.

12. Newitt, *Mozambique,* 25.

13. Munslow, "Maputo," 943.

14. Munslow, "Maputo."

15. James, *Mozambique,* 88.

16. Newitt, *Mozambique,* 4.

17. Newitt, *Mozambique,* 395.

18. Newitt, *Mozambique,* 469.

5

Cuisine and Traditional Dress

CUISINE

MOZAMBIQUE IS PRIMARILY an agricultural country. People farm and produce most of what they eat, especially millet, cassava, maize, bananas, rice, and cashew nuts. In addition, most of the poultry, beef, and milk consumed in the country is domestically produced. The surplus of what is farmed or produced is sold to help meet the basic financial needs of the household to buy foodstuffs from outside of the locality or imported from abroad. The availability of food for the majority of the citizenry is dependent on good weather conditions. This means that if rains fail or floods destroy crops the country faces famine and lost revenue. Nevertheless, Mozambicans are hard working and plant food crops all year round. Vegetables are grown in small gardens and poultry and related products and beef are produced domestically at the household level.

The country has interacted with the continents of Asia and Europe over the course of several centuries, and its cuisines reflect triple influences from within Mozambique as well as the two continents.[1] Significant in this aspect is the fact that the Portuguese introduced the current main food crops of maize and cassava from the Americas.[2] The Portuguese also introduced cashews, pineapples, and peanuts. Rice, ginger, oranges, lemons, and mangoes came from Asia, while millet is indigenous to Mozambique. The dietary situation in Mozambique reflects one's wealth and status in society as well as differing rural and urban lifestyles. On one hand the rural folks have a dietary pattern that reflects their daily struggle to eke out a living in the midst of poverty. Dissimilarly, the wealthy people who live in cities exhibit a dietary lifestyle that befits their status, which is usually patterned along Western lines. Most of the people in urban areas who do not have wealth are not necessarily better off than their rural counterparts when it comes to diet and access to food. At the same time there are invariably a few wealthy people in rural areas who live and eat well.

Those who are well off can easily afford three meals in a day. For the very wealthy, especially in cities, the meal is eaten in courses. The breakfast/dining table is formally set, and lace tablecloth and napkins are provided. Knives and forks are invariably used instead of fingers. Breakfast consists of cereal, hot tea or coffee, toasted bread, eggs, bacon, sausage, and a fruit. Lunch is equally heavy and is eaten either at home or in some hotel depending on the schedule of the person. The main dishes for lunch are rice, potatoes, and cornmeal. These are accompanied by beef, chicken, and fish stews. Fruit juices, sodas, or tea are the most popular nonalcoholic beverages. Wine and beer also are always available as for those who drink alcoholic beverages.

Dinner for the affluent begins with soup and ends with wine. The main dish might include Portuguese code steak or barbecued piles of freshly caught prawns, kingfish, or crab for those who like seafood. Chicken and beef dishes are always available. The chicken, beef, and seafood dishes are served with rice, cornmeal, or potatoes. Mozambican cuisines are spicy. Some dishes can be very "hot," especially if rubbed down with *piri-piri,* a fiery African chili sauce.[3] Dinner is usually a family affair where all members of the family share the table. However, friends are often invited or a visiting member of the extended family from the countryside might eat together with the host and his wife and children.

The dishes served in most of the high-class hotels in Maputo as well as in other cities are way beyond the income of most rural folks or the struggling middle class, who can hardly afford three multicourse meals a day. However, there are restaurants in most of the cities that serve good food at very reasonable prices. Fried chicken, fries, and soda would be half the price of what is asked in some of the high-class hotels. Such restaurants are usually full because they are affordable. There are also fast food places where one can buy a soda and cake or bread. The cities provide various alternatives for the urban dwellers depending on what one can afford. Indeed, the city of Maputo has restaurants that serve special cuisines: Ethiopian, Italian, Indian, and Portuguese. In contrast, those who live in rural areas have one big meal, dinner. This is because most members of the family are at home and all share in the family meal. Lunch is rarely a big family affair because both men and women are out working on the farm, herding, or walking to a market to sell or buy items, and children are away in school. As a result, lunch is invariably an individual meal.

The less-endowed families eat meat, but less frequently. Beef is widely available because it is sold in practically all the market centers, but it is expensive for some families. Those in rural areas usually hunt wild game, which is a rich source of meat for the rural households that have limited resources. Similarly, those who live adjacent to the ocean or rivers usually fish and consume part of what they get and sell the rest. Fish or beef is steamed, fried, or barbecued. Proximity to the ocean, lake, or river implies access to fish and other seafood, while settlement adjacent to a place with plentiful wild game means access to meat from hunting. The paradox here is that the game meat is quite expensive in the high-class hotels, which are frequented by the affluent.

Most rural Mozambicans grow cassava, millet, corn, rice, cashews, and peanuts and fruits such as mangoes, pineapples, oranges, and lemons. Of all these crops cassava is the most important because it constitutes the main diet for most Mozambicans. Cassava is drought resistant and grows in most parts of country. Growing it is less laborious than most crops because it requires less tending and weeding. It is a cheap source of carbohydrates. The various parts of the cassava plant are also used in variety of ways to make different cuisines. Because of these factors cassava is seen as the most vital crop in guaranteeing self-sufficiency in food. Its root can be boiled or roasted and consumed. The root can also be dried in the sun, then ground into flour and mixed with hot water to make porridge. When dried and grated it can also be mixed with either corn or millet or both and ground into flour, which can also be used in making porridge or bread. The leaves of the cassava are used as a vegetable, the same way spinach or collard greens are used. They can also be added to a mixture of corn and cassava flour and water to make yellow dough, which is then served in calabashes. In addition, roasted nuts as well as weak palm wine, called *shema,* are served to wash down the meal.[4]

Corn is also a very important crop in the diet of most people. Besides being ground into flour and used as explained in the preceding paragraph, corn can be steamed, roasted, and eaten alone or in combination with other food. It has calorific value similar to that of rice, yet it has higher amounts of protein, fat, and iron, and is less expensive than rice. Corn waste is used for feeding chickens. It is also commercially processed into flour and cooking oil. Mozambicans also use corn flour to make *sadza* or *nsima,* which is a type of softer porridge that is usually eaten once a day with meat, fish, or vegetables.[5] Mozambicans also grow a wide variety of beans that are steamed or fried and eaten in combination with other food. Beans are cherished because of their protein value.

Fruits are plentiful in Mozambique. Those in the rural areas grow and eat oranges, mangoes, bananas, and pineapples. Some of the surplus is sold in local markets, while the rest is purchased by traders who in turn sell it to the major towns at higher prices. Some fruits grow wild and can be gathered by anyone. This is usually what people do when they go out to hunt. Also, children helping with chores such as herding often gather and eat such fruits and carry some back home to share with family members.

Coastal Mozambicans eat a lot more seafood than do the hinterland communities. Similarly, cashew nuts, coconuts, and mangoes are readily available. The use of coconuts to spice the foods is common among the coastal communities. The Portuguese and Asians have also had a heavy influence. The Portuguese-style dish called *macaza,* which is shellfish skewed on bamboo twigs and grilled over open fire, is a popular delicacy.[6] The same is true of *bacalhao,* which is dried, salted fish mixed with vegetables. In the interior, the diet consists mainly of foods rich in starch and carbohydrates. Another delicacy of Portuguese influence is *matata,* which are clams cooked in port wine with finely chopped peanuts and tender young greens or fruits.[7] Similarly, in the interior, chicken heavily peppered and roasted on a grill is quite popular. It reflects a mix of African and Asian flavors, heavy pepper being associated with Indians and chicken an African delicacy.

CEREMONIES

Ceremonies such as birth, initiations, weddings, communal work, and death require special meals depending on the individuals involved. New mothers are usually taken care of by their sisters, aunts, or mother-in-law, who usually prepare a special meal. The emphasis is on regaining strength and ensuring that the mother is able to breastfeed her newborn baby. The meal consists of a wide array of cuisines, which include *nsima* with beef, chicken, or fish as well as nonalcoholic beverages. In the same vein, initiation from childhood to adulthood is a festive event, and the initiates are treated to a heavy meal. Among the Makua, for example, the initiates partake of chicken, but they are not supposed to eat its skin or break a bone.

Weddings are usually quite demanding in terms of the expenses. Depending on the economic means of the parties directly involved in the preparation of such ceremonies, several animals are slaughtered to feed guests that number in the hundreds—a lot of cooking is involved. Both alcoholic and nonalcoholic beverages are served. In the less-urban environments, traditional brew is cherished. Guests eat to their full and are entertained with music. Traditional artists perform. In the rural areas, the wedding is much more of a public event, and people in the locality attend if they are able to without necessarily being specially invited, as is the case in urban areas. This is not surprising because in urban areas the hosts must hire a hall and a catering firm and decide on cuisine that suits the needs of the guests. It is therefore a more expensive undertaking than in the rural areas, where the cuisine tends to be closely identified with the ethnic community.

Christmas is for many Mozambicans not only a religious day, but also one of sharing and festivity. Besides the heavy shopping and home decoration, Mozambicans prepare special meals for the occasion. While the cuisines are not dissimilar from what is usually eaten, even households that are economically challenged strive to slaughter chicken or purchase meat, fruit juices, and sodas as well as host other relatives and friends. As a result, the cooking is heavy. As opposed to initiations, weddings, and funerals, Christmas parties involve fewer people, because visitation is usually based on invitation. Also, the presentation of the meal in such a case tends to be much more leisurely and precise because it involves close family or friends.

Cuisines are sometimes determined by a religious specialist, especially for special ceremonies such as traditional treatments involving a sick person. The herbalist or diviner will determine the type of food to be eaten as well as the way in which it is to be cooked: boiled, roasted, or fried. The healer may recommend that a goat, sheep, or cow be slaughtered. Sometimes the recommendation is very specific in terms of the color and parts to be eaten. The word of the healer is generally final, because the food is for the specific purpose of helping a patient to recover.

The time spent on preparing a meal depends on the type of meal and the occasion. A meal for a few people within the homestead is less laborious, and a daily routine of gathering what is to be cooked is followed. In case of visitors from outside of the homestead or during special ceremonies, cooking is laborious, and the host invites other members of the family or clan to assist. The preparation of a meal can take several hours because a variety of cuisines is served. It is not uncommon to delegate the cooking so that one group focuses on a specific cuisine.

GENDER AND CULINARY DUTIES

Culinary duties in the traditional society were largely gender-specific. Women did and still do most of the cooking. Mothers and grandmothers train young girls to master and prepare various recipes. Young girls are expected to be actively involved in the preparation of a meal in one way or another. They observe what their older sisters do and as they come of age they assume such duties as preparing meals for a small group, then a much larger group. The pride of a mother is to see her daughter grow up as a responsible girl who will in the future be a responsible woman taking care of her family by performing her culinary duties. Meal schedules must be adhered to, especially dinnertime in households with infants and younger kids who are expected to go to sleep early.

In the rural areas, most of the cooking is done within the house. Some households have kitchens. However, during bright sunny days, women make hearths outside where they prepare their meals. Firewood is widely used by most people in the rural areas because access to electricity is for the most part unavailable. The situation is different in urban areas, where the use of firewood is not allowed in most of the middle- to upper-income residential areas. Electricity or gas stoves are widely used in urban areas. Some modern homes built of brick or concrete have built-in kitchens and accompanying facilities such as electric or gas stoves. Those who cannot afford electric or gas stoves usually use kerosene cookers, which are more economical.

Men too have a role to play during ceremonies, especially when a bull, goat, or sheep is to be slaughtered. Men usually do the slaughter. In situations where Moslems are among the visitors, a fellow Moslem is required to perform the task because they will not partake of beef from an animal that is not slaughtered by one of their own. After the slaughter of the animal, the men will divide the animal as directed and then have the women pick their share to cook. Men like to barbecue, and barbecuing is quite common during parties to commemorate special occasions. Some of the beef being barbecued may be rubbed with piri piri, but care is taken to ensure that those who do not enjoy piri piri are not inconvenienced.

The modern economy is blurring the traditional culinary gender divide. Young immigrants in the city are no longer bound by the gender-specific culinary duties. A single man prepares his own food. He determines what he wants to eat and how to prepare it. Men join culinary training institutions. Most of the big hotels employ men as chefs and servers. Furthermore, some families engage the services of a maid. This is the norm rather than the exception among households where the wife and husband are working and have children to be taken care of during their absence. In this case, the maid will be responsible for feeding the baby and making sure that other siblings eat well and at the right time. Maids are mostly young girls. However, middle-aged women are also infrequently hired. The maid lives with the family; however, the direct monetary compensation tends to be rather low.

BEVERAGES

Most important ceremonies are incomplete without beverages. In the traditional setting, beer was an indispensable drink that was consumed during ceremonies such as initiation, communal work, plentiful harvest, marriage, and death. The feedstock for traditional liquor is germinated maize that is dried, ground, and fermented with sugar for a week or so before being filtered. It can be drunk as such or further fermented and distilled to produce gin, which is quite strong. Heavy cooking, roasting, and the liberal flow of beer and gin are usually the norm during important ceremonies. A host who provides plenty of food and beer for visitors to eat and drink to their fill is usually praised, appreciated, and honored by the society. Such a host commands respect and is rarely faulted.

Among the Makua ethnic group local brew, *utheka,* was an indispensable drink when communal work, *ichiyao,* was undertaken by family members to help one of their own. The assigned communal task could be anything from cultivating or weeding to helping one construct a home. Besides utheka, the host was supposed to provide plenty of food for those who came to assist in the ichiyao. The utheka could only be taken after completion of the assigned task. Hence, the drinking spree was a way in which the community celebrated after a hard days work. The brew thus played a significant role in not only helping nurture ichiyao, but also the spirit of kinship in communal undertakings.

Traditional brews are also a source of income for some people who rely on the sales for their livelihood. The stronger the brew the better it is. This is because patrons can spend less and yet get satisfied. It is not uncommon for unscrupulous sellers to dilute strong gin with water to increase the quantity in their possession and the amount to be sold. Children below the age of 18 are defined as juveniles and are not supposed to partake of alcohol. Enforcement is problematic, especially where public nuisance is not reported. Furthermore, there is no strict way of enforcement because one is not supposed to show his/her identification before buying beer. At any rate those selling the alcoholic beverages are primarily focused on their business, not on law enforcement. Thus underage drinking is more rampant in urban areas than in rural areas. In the latter case, the traditional society tends to act as a check on such excesses because the community does not condone it. Underage drinking is frowned upon and stands condemned. While young people do it clandestinely, it is still unacceptable for a juvenile to be seen drunk or engaged in public nuisance under the influence of alcohol or drugs. Even for adults, society appreciates moderation in drinking. As a result, drunkards are resented because they give a bad name to the family or clan.

Shops and bars stock beer and wines produced in factories. Most of the wines and beers are imported into the country, especially from South Africa. While traditional brews are associated with rural folks or those of low income, the working middle class as well as the affluent mainly consume imported beer and wine. Thus, most hotels, bars, restaurants, and nightclubs serve imported beer and wine. Parties are incomplete without beer. For the affluent in major cities wine is part of a meal. Some stock beer and wine for their favored guests. Beer drinking is common among teens from affluent families.

It is one of the areas where tradition that forbade teens from drinking is generally disregarded and no longer tenable, although most parents still forbid and discourage their teenage sons and daughters from drinking.

Besides the alcoholic beverages, there are many varieties of soft drinks such as sodas and fruit juices. Most shops sell a wide variety of sodas including Fanta, Coca-Cola, Pepsi, and 7-Up. However, not everyone can afford to buy the drinks. Most families buy sodas when they have distinguished guests visiting or on special occasions. Sodas are not a common person's drink. Fruit juices such as orange, apple, and mango are sold in grocery stores. Once again, most people cannot afford such stocked fruit juices because of the cost. Instead, they eat fresh fruits that are available and affordable. In the major cities there are large grocery stores where one can buy all types of drinks ranging from imported wine and spirits to sodas and fruit juices. All restaurants serve tea, which is a popular drink and is very affordable. Tea is usually served with bread or donuts, biscuits, and cakes. Tea is not only a breakfast beverage; it can also be consumed at any time of the day. Coffee is another important beverage. There are numerous cafes in most of the major towns that serve coffee; however, it is less popular than tea. In sum, Mozambique has a wide array of both alcoholic and nonalcoholic beverages.

Religion is a factor influencing the type of beverage one drinks. Moslems do not partake of alcohol, but they have plenty of alternatives to choose from such as sodas, fruit juices, and tea. Similarly, some Christians are not in favor of drinking too much alcohol because it impairs one's judgment if the person becomes intoxicated, and a drunkard is likely to get involved in activities that are harmful to the body. Law forbids driving when drunk. Some denominations forbid the drinking of not only alcohol, but also some beverages that are thought to be stimulants. Followers of the Seventh Day Adventists, a Christian denomination, discourage the drinking of alcohol or coffee for purely a religious motive. Tea, fruit juices, and sodas are acceptable.

The onset of HIV/AIDS has led to public education to create awareness and discourage people from getting intoxicated. Intoxication impairs judgment and leads to recklessness that can result in illicit and unprotected sex. As a result, moderation in drinking is encouraged. Billboards that sensitize people to the dangers that one can get into if drunk are displayed at strategic points in towns and major roads. Nevertheless, people still frequent bars, nightclubs, and parties where they enjoy drinks. While some are cautious in terms of the company they keep during such occasions, others have yet to change their attitude. Furthermore, some start drinking at a relatively young age in the urban areas where societal control is less pronounced. As more young people move to the cities in search of employment opportunities, they become independent and make decisions outside the influence of their traditional societies. Popular urban culture, television and radio, and aggressive marketing by companies that sell alcoholic drinks have enormous influence on the type of drink the young people resort to when they begin drinking.

While the impact of civil war on Mozambican politics and economy was discussed in chapter one, it is important to note that the war also affected Mozambican traditional life in many ways, especially in the types of food as well as culinary patterns. Those who were forced to flee their homes found themselves as refugees in the neighboring countries of Malawi, Zambia, Swaziland, Tanzania, and Zimbabwe.[8] As refugees, Mozambicans had to partake of food that was provided by their hosts or international agencies that provided relief for their sustenance. They relished some of the cuisines provided, while others were less cherished because of the way the meals were prepared.[9]

TRADITIONAL DRESS

Clothing represents the various cultural influences that have contributed to the evolution and development of Mozambique as a nation: African, European, and Islamic. Mozambique does not have a national dress. Those who work for the government as well as banking institutions wear Western style outfits, with men's preference being suits, and women's dresses cut in European styles. Clothing stores sell pretailored styles, and customers buy what fits them. Alternatively, some stores sell clothing material, which is then tailor-made depending on what the customer wants. For men's suits and women's formal dresses, the preferred colors are usually dark. People looking for employment in the formal sector (i.e., white-collar jobs in the public or private sector) are required to be formally dressed, preferably in a suit, during a job interview. Also, during certain functions such as board meetings, a gathering in major hotel, or a meeting with a senior official for formal discussion one is required to be formally dressed.

Dress not only performs the vital function of protecting the body, but it also reveals one's identity, gender, religion, status, and nationality. Priests wear special clothes. In the traditional society, diviners who led the community in the performance of certain rituals had special clothing that showed their power and special status in society. If occasion demanded, they would even wear masks to mystify their presence and role by imitating a past ancestor. The attire was a traditionally woven cloth covered with furs or feathers for the occasion pertaining to the ritual. Dress and culture were closely linked. Similarly, Moslem and Christian leaders adorn themselves with special dress that befits the ritual that they preside over. Dress also signifies one's profession in some cases, such as the police, members of the military, or nurses. Similarly, dress is used to identify a group set aside from society for the purpose of incarceration as in the case of prisons.

Most of the citizenry are less formal in their dressing. Most men prefer trousers with a shirt and jacket or a coat. The shirt/jacket/coat need not match the trousers, especially in terms of color. The colors tend to be bright and the clothing a mosaic of various patterns. Women wear long, striped garments. Miniskirts or tight trousers for women are frowned upon in some rural areas. Most women in rural areas wear head cloths. They are less preoccupied with hairdos because of certain tasks they perform, such as carrying baskets, firewood, or pots on their heads. Theirs is a life of struggle pertaining to chores of fending for basic family needs. The income and time to invest in hairdos are nonexistent. While some women in urban areas still wear head cloths, most are inclined to have their hair done at the many salons that charge money. There are salons where one can have her hair done at a reasonably cheap price, while others are fairly expensive and are patronized by clients who can afford the higher prices. The style and cost of a woman's hairdo is an indication of her class or status. Most working-class women opt for a hairdo instead of a head cloth. Women from affluent families wear hats, which is a sign of affluence and dignity and is usually worn with matching clothing and shoes. They also wear rings, necklaces, bracelets, and earrings in silver and gold.

Long white robes, turbans, and veils are the preferred and popular clothing for Muslim men and women, who constitute 20 percent of the Mozabican population. Men wear turbans, while women wear veils. Some Muslim women wear clothing that completely covers the body, except for the eyes. The preferred color is black, in contrast to the white robes worn by the men. It should be emphasized that many Muslim men dress formally just like other non-Muslim men in the country. Asian men's attire is in many ways similar to that worn by other non-Muslim men: suits, trousers, jackets, and/or coats. On the other hand, Asian women wear long, black, or colored silk dresses, sometimes with material wrapped around the body under the arms and over one shoulder.

In the traditional society African royalty usually donned more expensive attire, either imported or locally produced, to show their status and power in society. This included objects that were decorated with beads, ivory, special goods, bronze, or silver. The fundamental difference is that in today's Mozambique, and indeed all of Africa, there has been a shift in power and wealth away from the traditional rulers to the new elite identified by their education, wealth, and status in the modern economy as well as state system.

Body adornment was an important fact of life in traditional society. Scarification and tattooing helped define one's identity as well as beauty.

Adornment was closely related to art in some societies, especially among the Makonde, who were renowned for the body art. Besides scarifications and tattoos, which were elaborate and formed geometric proportions, filing of teeth as well as wearing of lip plugs were marks of identity among the Makonde.[10]

The practices of filing teeth and wearing lip plugs are no longer undertaken; they have disappeared. This demonstrates the dynamic nature of cultural traditions. Communities constantly engage in dialogue with their traditions, and in the process ones that have outlived their usefulness are discarded. The elegance, beauty, and identity that were the hallmarks of filing teeth and lip plugs are thus no longer in vogue. In a sense, what constitutes beauty and elegance is subject to time and change.

The nature and extent of body adornments have changed. They are not as elaborate as they were in traditional society. The marks are now confined to only the face. As result, even those who reside in the rural areas are no longer enthusiastic about traditional scarifications and tattoos. As the meaning and context of dress, beauty, and adornment shifts, so Mozambicans' attitude toward traditional ways of dressing, beauty, and adornment are changing. Those who have resources now visit beauticians where they can get quality service to help them look presentable as defined by modern society. School children are required to wear uniforms. Fancy clothing is discouraged and unacceptable in school. School uniforms identify the youth in primary and secondary schools as belonging to a group of youths that is associated with an educational institution. Within the school, it allows the students to see themselves as equal, thereby minimizing the problem of poor vs. rich children when students are allowed to dress as they deem fit. In such cases, students from poor families are inclined to see themselves as less fortunate, a development that can have an adverse impact on their learning.

The type and style of uniform is simple and determined by the principal in consultation with the parents. Each school has its uniform, although it is possible to have more than one school with the same uniform. But that is rare, especially in the case of adjacent schools. The uniform is usually a short-sleeved shirt and a pair of shorts for boys and a simple cotton dress for girls that reaches the knee. Some of the primary school students in rural areas do not wear shoes. For some struggling families, shoes are a luxury they cannot afford. Most children in urban primary schools do wear shoes. Teachers always enforce the uniform code, including the cleanliness. The children are supposed to shave their head and/or ensure that their hair is trimmed. Elaborate hairdos are unacceptable for both boys and girls.

Western influence on fashion in Mozambique cannot be overemphasized. T-shirts or *dashikis* are widely worn by Mozambicans, and so are pullover shirts. Suits are the preferred clothing when it comes to corporate or government officials. Caps and sunglasses are cherished by the youth of Mozambique. A number of factors explain the Western impact on fashion in Mozambique. First, the large importation of secondhand/used clothing from the West has made cheaply priced clothing readily available. As a result, most Mozambicans can purchase practically everything from shoes and socks to suits and ties. Weaving as it was practiced in the traditional society is uncompetitive today with developments in technology. The modern textile technology produces finer and better materials in huge quantities at a much faster rate than traditional weaving techniques, and it is not surprising therefore that the Western influence on fashion looms large over society.

In addition, the media tends to focus on the news and popular culture of the West. That focus has had its impact on the country, especially among the youths, with specific reference to dress, music, and hairstyle. The result is that Western fashion is increasingly being embraced by the young as many of them view the fashions emanating from the West as representing modernity. Furthermore, with globalization and the movement of goods and ideas, it is fashionable to wear a T-shirt with an Addidas imprint or a Milan Soccer Club cap. Although dressing in Mozambique represents the various cultural influences that have impacted the country in the last couple of centuries, there is no doubt that the impact of the West has been disproportionately great.

NOTES

1. Bea Sandler, et al., *The African Cookbook* (New York: Carol Publishing Group, 1993).

2. R. S. James, *Places and Peoples of the World: Mozambique* (New York and Philadelphia: Chelsea Press, 1988), 66–67.

3. Bea Sandler, *The African Cookbook,* 72.

4. R. S. James, *Mozambique,* 67.

5. Mario Joaquim Azevedo, *Tragedy and Triumph: Mozambique Refugees in South Africa, 1977–2001* (Portsmouth, NH: Heinemann, 2002), 73.

6. R. S. James, *Mozambique,* 68.

7. R. S. James, *Mozambique,* 68.

8. For a detailed treatment of this theme of displacement and refugee life outside of Mozambique, see Mario Joaquim Azevedo, *Tragedy and Triumph* and Margaret Hall and Tom Young, *Confronting Leviathan: Mozambique since Independence* (Athens: Ohio University Press, 1997).

9. Mario Joaquim Azevedo, *Tragedy and Triumph,* 72–77.

10. John Stoner, *Makonde* (New York: Rosen Publishing Group, 1998), 38–40.

Mozambique was heavily mined during the liberation and civil wars that plagued the country for more than three decades. Deactivating the landmines is a slow, risky, and painstaking exercise. This officer is using a metal detector to identify and deactivate a landmine. Photo by Mike DuBose, United Methodist News Service.

The use of dogs in identifying landmines is quite common because it minimizes the loss of limbs and lives. Photo by Mike DuBose, United Methodist News Service.

Thousands of people lost limbs, both during the wars and after, especially during the process of deactivating landmines. Photo by Mike DuBose, United Methodist News Service.

This ruined building is a manifestation of the ravages of war. The building housed Eduardo Mondlane's office at Cambine when it was a mission station. Photo by Mike DuBose, United Methodist News Service.

Mozambicans honor their war heroes. This monument was built in honor of Mozambican veterans. Courtesy of Dan and Robin Been, Missionaries in Mozambique.

Xai-Xai President Joaquim Chissano High School is one of the most modern high schools in the country. Courtesy of The Mozambique Initiative—Missouri Conference United Methodist Church.

These students must wear uniforms, a cost that prohibits some children from attending school. Photo by Mike DuBose, United Methodist News Service.

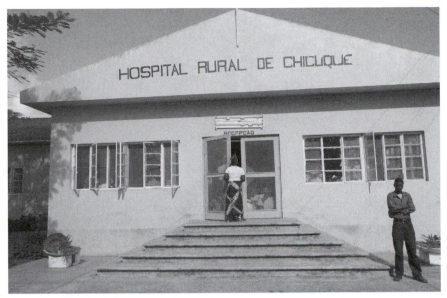

UMC built Chicuque Rural Hospital, which has a 163-bed capacity and serves about 500,000 people. Courtesy of The Mozambique Initiative—Missouri Conference United Methodist Church.

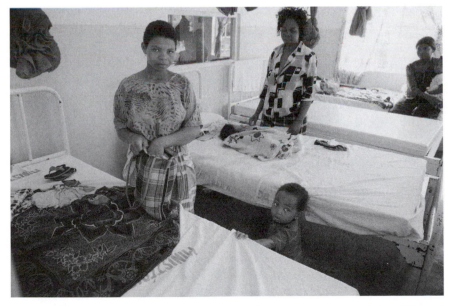

Inpatients at Chicuque Rural Hospital. Courtesy of The Mozambique Initiative—Missouri Conference United Methodist Church.

Families are usually forced to walk long distances in search of clean drinking water. This water project is being commissioned to help the local people access clean drinking water. Photo by Mike DuBose, United Methodist News Service.

UMC's Living Water Society in Mozambique drilled this well in order to help local people have access to clean drinking water. Photo by Mike DuBose, United Methodist News Service.

The government policy of encouraging private investment has contributed to the growth of industries as this modern industrial complex in Maputo shows. Courtesy of The Mozambique Initiative—Missouri Conference United Methodist Church.

Local artisans play an important role in the Mozambican economy. These products are sold in local markets. Photo by Mike DuBose, United Methodist News Service.

Fishing is an important economic activity because fish is a local delicacy as well as a commodity for export. It is mostly men who go out to sea to fish. Photo by Mike DuBose, United Methodist News Service.

Poultry farm at Cambine. Photo by Mike DuBose, United Methodist News Service.

Fresh vegetables, fruits, and eggs are usually sold in such open-air markets. Courtesy of Dan and Robin Been, Missionaries in Mozambique.

Celebrating birthdays are common among the middle- and upper-income families, especially in the cities. Courtesy of PAO Photos.

Most affluent people usually build very decent modern homes not only in cities but also in rural areas. Courtesy of PAO Photos.

This building is in Nampula city. Notice the huge dish receivers mounted on the top of the building for accessing radio and television networks. Courtesy of Dan and Robin Been, Missionaries in Mozambique.

A view of Maputo Bay. Courtesy of The Mozambique Initiative—Missouri Conference United Methodist Church.

Bringing up a child is the responsibility of both the young and old. This girl is helping the mother by playing with her sibling after school. Courtesy of PAO Photos.

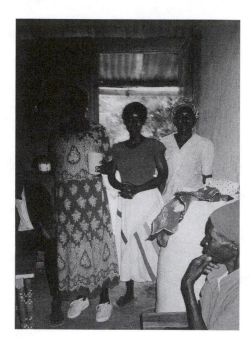

In traditional African society, old age is appreciated and respected. It is the duty of children to take care of the elderly. Daughters-in-law are serving this grandmother. Courtesy of PAO Photos.

This curio shop in Maputo displays a wide array of Mozambican art. Courtesy of The Mozambique Initiative—Missouri Conference United Methodist Church.

Vendors sell locally produced bags and hats at very affordable rates. Courtesy of The Mozambique Initiative—Missouri Conference United Methodist Church.

Music and dance is incomplete without traditional instruments. These instruments are from Nampula province. Courtesy of Dan and Robin Been, Missionaries in Mozambique.

Drums perform several important functions in most Mozambican societies. Young people also appreciate the significance of the drum as an instrument of entertainment. Courtesy of The Mozambique Initiative—Missouri Conference United Methodist Church.

In most churches, sermons are given in local languages, and choirs use traditional instruments. Photo by Mike DuBose, United Methodist News Service.

With a portable radio, cassette, or CD players, not only are young people able to enjoy favorite music but also to listen to news broadcasts. Courtesy of PAO Photos.

6

Gender Roles, Marriage, and Family

THE FAMILY IS a very important institution in Mozambican society. It is where a child is born, nurtured, and sensitized to social mores as well as aspects of education before being initiated into adulthood. After initiation one is expected to marry, raise a family, and contribute to the development of the wider community. All communities in Mozambique recognize the family as not only a biological unit, but also as a social and economic organization. Its nature and structure defines domestic roles based on age and gender. Members of a family may be related by blood; marriage and adoption are two other significant ways by which family members are related. Belonging to a family brings shared benefits and responsibilities. In the traditional Mozambican society every individual had a vital role to play in the betterment of society. As a result, the individual stood to reap the benefits of being a member of the family. The family was there for you because you were there for the family. It was the responsibility of all members of the family to work for common good during both good and bad times, especially sickness, and death.

Two issues are considered critical to the growth and development of society. Of the two, the ability of society to reproduce its next generation was and still is the most significant. A society that is unable to reproduce itself cannot guarantee its survival beyond the next couple of generations. In this regard, Mozambican societies considered marriage to be one of the most important stages in an individual's life. It has far-reaching repercussions on the future of not only the individuals concerned, but also for the extended family, lineage, and wider community. Through marriage and procreation, the family and society are assured of a future beyond the present generation. The other critical issue, hard work, was and still is cherished and highly valued. This calls for organizing chores to ensure the participation of all members of the family. Every individual in the family has a specific role to play. In the traditional society men performed tasks that were determined for them by the society. Similarly, women too had their duties prescribed.

This chapter examines the various aspects of familial life, especially marriage, the kinship system, and gender roles, in the context of the growth and development of contemporary Mozambican societies. Mozambicans have not been immune to changes brought on by education, urbanization, migration, and religion. Consequently, familial life is examined against the backdrop of these various changes that have enormously impacted marriage, gender relations, and household division of labor. The chapter addresses the waning customs and cultures of the past but that still show some presence in parts of the country, albeit on a much smaller and narrower scale than was the case a couple of generations ago. Similarly, in looking at changes that are impacting society in the course of present times, it can be seen that change in any community is never homogenous over a given geographical, political, or economic landscape, and Mozambique is no exception to this general trend.

MARRIAGE

Marriage in contemporary Mozambique is, by and large, strictly understood as a union between two people of the opposite sex. It is about love and companionship. Sexual intercourse is an important aspect of this love and companionship. Intercourse between people of the same sex is strictly forbidden, because procreation is a significant factor in a marital relationship. Yet procreation can only result from the union between two people of the opposite sex. It is also the only way by which a society reproduces itself to ensure its continued existence.

Traditional society suppresses romantic feelings toward people of the same sex through elaborate education that start at infancy and reaches its climax during initiation from childhood to adulthood. Even where initiation is not undertaken in the traditional way because of a family residing outside of rural areas where familial and communal ties are strong, discussions on love and sexual companionship are strictly conducted in the context of heterosexual relationships.

Mozambican societies place an exceptionally high value both on heterosexual marriage and on having children. Marriage is therefore accepted as a normal rhythm of life that brings together not just two individuals, but also two families. Sex is the gift of a relationship that exemplifies the depth and riches of individuals bonded together by marriage. It deepens and strengthens the marital relationship. As a result of sexual intercourse, conception usually occurs and children are born. Thus, one of the major purposes of marriage is procreation, because one's own being is immortalized—the person does not only live in the present, but also in the future. The legacy bequeathed to the individual by his ancestors is continued after death through procreation. The family name is perpetuated and the link between ancestors and the living assured. Without children the family dies off.

A childless marriage is considered a misfortune. The couples involved always try to do all they can by visiting traditional healers as well as diviners to help identify the problem and offer help. Procreation and marriage are closely tied together because the two provide spiritual continuity as well as material well-being. The more descendants one has, the better off one is considered and the more one is assured of being immortalized after death. This triad of marriage, procreation, and descendants explains the pride of place marriage occupies in Mozambican society.

It is against the foregoing backdrop that polygyny, marrying more than one wife, is accepted by Mozambican societies. Polygyny is a safeguard against childlessness in the family. The burden of childlessness weighs more heavily on women rather than men. A man could marry an additional wife to dispense with the stigma of not having children, but such an alternative is not readily available for a woman. This is not to suggest that there are not men who are unable to father children for whatever reason. However, in such cases making that determination is not easy. As a result, it is the woman who shoulders the burden and pain of infertility if the couple is unable to have a child.

Polygyny is also significant because of the contribution of women's labor to the wealth of the households. In addition, more wives means more children, which increases the amount of labor at the disposal of the household. Since most of these societies were and still are predominantly agricultural, labor is critical for the sustenance of the economy of households. Even among the Yao, who were predominantly long-distance traders, labor was still a critical factor.[1] While some personnel traversed long distances in search of trade items, many more remained at home to ensure the nurturance of children, protect the community, and produce basic agricultural product. Furthermore, polygyny was accepted and widely practiced among Moslems and so was the norm rather than the exception across the predominantly Moslem Mozambican society.

High infant mortality rates also contribute to the high number of polygynous marriages. Few children survive into adulthood. In this regard, polygyny serves to ensure that as many children as possible survive infancy. It makes sense to many people who live in traditional society that having more children ensures that at least a few survive into adulthood. Since children are valued, utmost care is taken to ensure that they survive. However, this cannot be guaranteed, since infant mortality rates remain quite high due to the many diseases affecting most households in the absence of modern healthcare facilities.

Furthermore, polygyny was acceptable in traditional society, and still is, because modern family planning methods are either rare or not acceptable to some people. Instead, couples rely on taboos that prohibit engaging in sexual intercourse for an extended period of time when a woman is still nursing a baby. Such periods vary, but can extend for up to three years. With strict rules against extramarital sex, most men resort to marrying a second or third wife. Polygyny is thus seen as a safeguard against infidelity. It is seen as a moral choice that is not frowned upon, because having mistresses or cohabiting is considered immoral and unacceptable. It is considered morally upright to accept responsibility and make known one's lover, a requirement that means bringing the woman home as a wife. Indeed, among the Muslims extramarital sex stands condemned, and there are serious penalties, but polygyny is morally accepted and sanctioned by the faith.

Thus, an adult in love has to declare his position for the family to know. The significance of this openness and sincerity ensures that children born to a couple are not considered illegitimate, because the father is known. It gives the offspring a sense of belonging to a specific family, lineage, clan, and community. This is important, especially when one or both parents pass away. It helps to prevent the problem of destitution that characterizes modern Mozambican society, especially in the urban areas. A child must have a father and a mother.

Polygyny carries heavy responsibility. A polygynous husband has the responsibility of taking care of the family. It is unacceptable to marry additional wives without the necessary support system. Most of those who engage in polygynous marriages are people of means because of the bride wealth, which is a marriage gift paid to the family of the bride. The exchange of bride wealth is an important ingredient of marriage negotiations. Upon the decision of marriage, the family of the bridegroom is supposed to pay the bride's family bride wealth, *lobola*.[2] The bride wealth is usually paid in cattle in various stages, and thus solemnizes the marriage. This means that those families that have daughters stand to gain from the payment of lobola. In contrast, the bridegroom's family loses cattle. Girls are cherished because the transfer of lobola gives the bride's family a chance to accumulate livestock, which is a valuable source of wealth. It is important to note that bride wealth is not the buying of a wife, as is erroneously portrayed in the West. It is compensation to the bride's family for the loss of her labor that is going to benefit the bridegroom's family. It formalizes the marriage and unites the two families.

Elaborate arrangements and negotiations precede the formalization of any marriage. Marriage is not marked by the one-day event of a wedding. It starts long before the day of marriage and includes a series of steps that continues even after the bride has moved to the bridegroom's home or vice versa.[3] Both parties usually scrutinize the history of the families of both the bride and bridegroom. This is considered important to ensure that debilitating diseases are not introduced into a family through marriage. It also helps to check on situations such as infertility. It is believed that families with rare cases of infertility would be unlikely to have girls that would be incapable of having children. While these background checks are never perfect, they show the seriousness with which marriage is taken by society.

The idea of prearranged marriages or a go-between—an individual who acts as a link between the bride and bridegroom's families and knows both parties well—must be viewed in this context of trying to ensure that the individuals as well as the families involved are well informed. One ought to look at these developments pertaining to marriage preparation in the positive light of the social meaning of marriage and family life. Contracting a marriage means more than two people meeting and making the decision to marry. The families from both sides are heavily involved in the marriage preparations. Indeed, one of the important functions of marriage is to widen the network of relatives by uniting two groups. It is in the best interest of the family, lineage, and clan that all information pertaining to the two families be assembled as a safeguard against last-minute or future surprises. It is these aspects of marriage preparation that help to minimize divorce in traditional society. If problems develop, the couple cannot make the unilateral decision to divorce; the relatives would come in to find the cause of the problem and help to resolve it before it gets out of control. Divorce brings not only misery to the children, but also shame to the families of both the wife and husband. It shows that they have failed in one way or another to ensure the stability of the institution of marriage. But as will be discussed in the last section of this chapter, single motherhood is not uncommon.

Traditional marriages also generally record low divorce rate because of the elaborate education that the potential bride and bridegroom go through before entering the institution of marriage. In this regard, traditional education plays an instrumental role in preparing youths for this very important stage in their lives. The Swahili proverb that the way you bring up a child is the way it grows up holds true among many Mozambican societies. Traditional education is not only to be acquired, but also to be lived. Hence preparation and education on matters pertaining to marriage is a key element in the knowledge that is imparted to initiates during their initiation ceremony, which marks their graduation from childhood to adulthood.

In the traditional Makonde society, boys and girls were given instructions about sex, marriage, and men's and women's duties in the society. Girls were usually considered ready for initiation and marriage at puberty. After initiation, a person called the *mnobo* assisted the new adults.[4] The mnobo had great influence over the behaviors of the new initiates and was expected to guide them through the new life of adulthood. This helped the initiates to assume the responsibilities of adulthood and family life by a common understanding of the essential elements of what it meant to be a wife, husband, mother, and father. These preparations coupled with the fact that both families were involved in marriage arrangements and the payment of bride wealth helped to create marital stability. In case of disagreement between the couples, divorce was not readily available on demand. Where the marriage had been blessed with children, divorce was rarely sanctioned.

LINEAGE AND DESCENT

Several families who share a common descent constitute a lineage. A lineage emphasizes a genealogical link. Just as in the case of family, members of a lineage tend to share certain features, such as a perceived ancestor, that unite the various family clusters that constitute it. Common or shared names, totems, and taboos characterize a lineage. Intralineage marriage is rare and sometimes strictly forbidden. In turn, several lineages make up a clan, which is a much larger unit. Intra- and interclan marriages are the norm. This shows that blood relations in such cases are either very weak or nonexistent. The various clans make up an ethnic group. At most of these levels, especially the clan and ethnic group, the most important issue is not its homogeneity, but rather its composition and how it came to be. Mozambican societies have been dynamic because of migration, interethnic marriages, and conquest. As a result, it is a misnomer to speak of a pure ethnic group, since ethnicity is an identity that is forged in the course of history to further a common cause for its membership. An ethnic group is therefore an amalgam of various elements whose ancestors at one point or another perhaps spoke different languages and even cherished different cultural traditions and economic lifestyles.[5]

Yet despite the foregoing diversity, common language, initiation rites, facial marks, and shared history of survivability all combine to present the impression of homogeneity. This image could not be further from the truth, though. Contrary to popular portrayals of homogeneity, lineages, clans, and ethnic groups are continually reforming. They are not static and unchanging. Usually, a clan or ethnic community incorporates many diverse groups that can hardly claim a common ancestry. This portrayal of homogeneity serves a very important function in securing land rights. It is commonly believed that the person who pioneered land and his/her unilineal descendants has total claim on the parcel in perpetuity, so the claim to that land is usually supported by reference to genealogy based on ancestry. Groups that come later are absorbed and find their claim by reference to the original lineage or clan.

Most Mozambican communities display pattern of unilineal descent, which is through one side of the parental generation. In unilineal pattern, descent can be either matrilineal or patrilineal, but not both. This is in contrast to bilineal descent, whereby an individual traces his ancestry through both sides of parental generation, as is usually the case in the United States. The Makonde are a matrilineal society.[6] They trace their origins and ancestry through their mothers' families rather than their fathers, as opposed to most of the communities who live south of the Zambezi River. The Tonga, the Yao, and the Chewa are also matrilineal.[7] In contrast to the matrilineal societies, the Karanga, the Chopi, and the Shona are patrilineal and trace their ancestry through the father. It is important to point out that the terms matrilineal and patrilineal are not necessarily about power. The two are distinct from matriarchy and patriarchy, which are directly related to authority and the exercise of power.[8]

Nevertheless, the type of descent, whether matrilineal or patrilineal, has a direct bearing on land ownership as well as residence patterns. It was the female lineages that owned land in matrilineal Makonde society. When a man got married, he went to live on the land that belonged to his wife's family. Relationships were traced in the female line. In the case of polygyny, he moved between the households of several wives. In matrilineal societies, husbands usually had less power. It was the wife's family that handled matters pertaining to inheritance of property. The converse was true in patrilineal societies, where it was the man's family that handled property issues. Relationships were traced in the male line.

SOCIALIZATION

Socialization is significant in all stages of life: childhood, teenage, and adulthood. Children are socialized to fit into society and accept its values. It is through socialization that the child acquires knowledge, skills, and suppositions that enable them to participate as active members of the society. For most of the Mozambican societies, parent-child contact is important during the first couple of years. Attachment to parents is emphasized so that the parent-child bond is strengthened as the child grows. Exceptionally high value is placed not only on having children, but also on the intensive care that is provided during the infancy period.

It is also noteworthy that customary child-care practices are largely influenced by concern for the health and survival of the infant. Babyhood is quite challenging to the parents because of the high infant mortality rates. Prolonged and intensive breast-feeding and the taboos that prohibit engaging in sexual intercourse when a woman is still nursing a baby serve to ensure that there is a long birth interval so that the mother can take care of the baby. Among the Tonga, it takes two to three years to wean children from the breast. This preoccupation with the well-being of the child is widespread in Mozambique. Most children in traditional society wear amulets, which are not just for decorative purposes but are also of medicinal value. The amulets are supposed to protect the child from disease and harm. Children's special needs thus call for careful nurturance and protection.

Relatives are many; within the homestead one might see a sister, brother, cousin, aunt, uncle, grandmother, and grandfather. The existence of many children in the homestead because of the polygynous nature of the families ensures that older children socialize the child as well. An aunt or uncle deserves as much respect as one's parents. The child is socialized into accepting the extended family. There is strict emphasis on compliance and obedience to the parents as well as to other family members. Children are taught to respect their seniors. To argue with a parent is considered rude. To challenge the wisdom of elders is considered an act of defiance.

Besides their peers, girls are supposed to spend more time with their mothers and grandmothers. This is to help socialize them into chores that they are supposed to undertake as teenagers, and later wives and mothers. This socialization process takes various forms: direct involvement in practical tasks such as drawing water from the river, fetching firewood, and cooking as well as being told stories, fables, folktales, proverbs, and legends. Inspired by these various forms of instructions, girls strive to perform at their best. Individual success is a source of pride not only for the parents, but also the grandparents. A family and lineage that produce hardworking and well-behaved girls are usually admired across the land.

Education in traditional society is not only gender specific, but also task oriented. Boys too are socialized into tasks that they are expected to perform. In this regard, they spend more time with their peers, older boys, and grandfathers. Initiation ceremonies crown an education process that begins during the infancy stages. In this way, young people coming of age are prepared to take their rightful place in society. They are expected to be good warriors who can defend the society well, exhibit good manners toward their elders, respect their wives, and be hard working and provide for the households. Such qualities usually endear the young man to many girls.

Discipline is not just the preserve of the parents. Elder sisters and brothers as well as aunts and uncles also share in the responsibility of ensuring that children grow up respecting seniors and behaving responsibly as members of the society. The family and community cherish children who are easy to manage and are productive members of society. Misbehavior and making unnecessary demands is forbidden. A rebellious child reflects badly not only on the parents, but also on the extended family. It shows that the parents and community failed to bring up the child to love and appreciate the cultural norms of respect, compliance, and obedience.

It takes a village to bring up and socialize the child into the community. Nothing illustrates this more than the fact that children are sometimes allowed to spend holidays with relatives such as aunts, uncles, or grandparents who live away from the child's home. The children are shown in a practical way the nature and extent of familial and kinship relations. They get to know that they are part of a wide network of relatives who are as important as the immediate family of father, mother, and siblings. Such networks are useful in case of calamities when a child loses one or both parents and is forced to relocate to live with relatives who will be responsible for his or her upbringing. The parents exhibit less of the possessiveness over children that characterizes Western society.

That adolescence brings with it challenges that ought to be handled carefully is appreciated by the society. Indeed, the initiation ceremonies that mark the transition from childhood to adulthood are primarily meant to address some of these challenges. Instructions during initiation focus on conduct and behavior as well as duties and responsibilities on the part of the initiate for his /her own good and for the best interests of entire community. The physical act of circumcision is usually a manifestation of the fact that the individual has gone through all the instructions required of an adult. The physical act is on the individual, but the instructions will have enormous impact on the way the initiate relates to family and society. A person is supposed to look beyond the self. The individual is socialized to be there for others. Unity is strength.

Kinship and family interests sometime take precedence over individual interests. Young people who go through the process of initiation from childhood to adulthood are taught that life is worth living because the society is there for them in good and bad times. They bond together as members of the same age-grade. They have come of age as a group, been taught the historical information about the cultural group and its rituals, and been united by the rite that they have all gone through. In due course they are supposed to marry and start raising family. With the passage of time they will become elders taking over from the generation that preceded them in the initiation ceremony. Kinship networks are still a significant factor in contemporary economy and politics. Wage employment and voting patterns are still heavily influenced by familial and kinship ties.

Seniority in age is respected and admired. This is because old age is associated with wisdom. Senior citizens are therefore accorded due respect because they are custodians of societal values. Their counsel is usually sought during times of crisis. They should not be angered because their curse could ruin one's future. However, the respect and admiration also come with certain responsibilities. As an elder, an individual is supposed to be unemotional, sober, and focused during crisis or stressful times. As an arbiter, an elder has to be candid and sincere in providing counsel. Also, as either father and grandfather, or mother and grandmother, the elder is supposed to be above partisan differences for his word and counsel to be accorded due respect and recognition. He is not supposed to engage in gossip. Thus, while in general seniority is synonymous with honor, respect, admiration, and wisdom, it is one's ability to manifest these qualities in old age that gives an individual elevated status in society.

Families strive to take good care of senior citizens because it sets a good example for young people. By treating their elders well, parents send a message to their children that they too would like to be accorded that honor, respect, and good treatment in old age. Indeed, one of the important reasons for procreation in traditional society was to have somebody to look after you in old age. Children brought up well were considered an asset. It was considered rude for a young man to sit down while an old person was standing. The young person was supposed to give up a seat for the old person as a sign of respect. The parents themselves must set a good example by respecting and taking care of their own parents. When children see that their grandparents are treated well, they learn by example that they too are expected to take care of their parents in old age.

The elder is the pillar of both the nuclear and extended family. Being the eldest living male descendant of the eldest son of the founder of the lineage, he is the link between the living and ancestors. He is supposed to unite the family so that the unity survives his death. He reinforces kinship ideology, maintains peace, and presides over family gatherings, during which period he keeps members within bounds by insisting on customs, laws, and traditional observances. He helps to socialize members of the family, immediate and extended, into the ways of the group. He represents the family whenever there are communal lineage meetings. In this way elders unite family and kinship members. In their oral will, in the presence of other elders, they provide guidance on how land will be parceled out among family members, appeal for unity among family and kinship members, and pass the baton of leadership to the next patriarch of the family.

Thus all members of the society take socialization seriously. That role transcends age and gender. This is because socialization contributes to cohesion and harmony within society. Hence siblings, mothers, fathers, and elders all have specific roles to play. Socialization is about making use of the past in the present to shape the future. As will be explained in the last section of this chapter, the stress on the traditional socialization process brought on by modern influences has greatly contributed to the erosion of the long-cherished traditions that welded society together.

FAMILY AND GENDER ROLES

Work is highly valued across the entire Mozambican society. It is considered honorable and is the only means through which people produce food, trade, build homes, raise their livestock, and defend their communities in case of attack. The need to work is instilled in all children from an early age regardless of gender. At the household level everybody has a contribution to make towards the family workload. Laziness is condemned, and an indolent person has no honor. Such an individual is the subject of gossip, scorn, and shame. A lazy person is a disgrace to the family and lineage. It is not uncommon to find such people socially stigmatized and ignored by the society. In contrast, a hard-working person is a source of inspiration for young people and brings pride to the family, both immediate and extended.

Roles are hierarchically organized and based on age and gender. The youngest children perform menial tasks. They could be asked to go and bring an item that is not within reach to the parents, or sent on a short errand to take something to a neighbor. Similarly, they could be asked to look after their younger siblings when the parents are out for a couple of hours doing garden work or going to the marketplace. Through such menial tasks, children are taught to appreciate the value of work and obedience to their parents if and when asked to perform certain responsibilities. It is important to note that the distinction based on gender in carrying out tasks is less pronounced at the young age of less than four years. Rather, the emphasis is on commitment and appreciation of work in society.

As children came of age, tasks become much more gender specific. Girls perform duties that are more domestically oriented: fetching firewood, drawing water from the river or well, gardening, gathering food, and cooking. Usually, young girls are helped in conducting these duties by their older siblings as well as mothers, aunts, and grandmothers. They are taught by example and deed how to perform those tasks that define womanhood in traditional society: taking care of the household, nurturing children, cooking good food, and farming or trading. In their teenage years, girls go through an initiation ceremony, during which period their role in society is emphasized. Marriage usually takes place after initiation based on the principle that their training from childhood to adulthood prepared them to be responsible wives and mothers.

Boys received training that is reflective of tasks they are supposed to perform in traditional society. Boys were introduced to herding, hunting, and warfare games in their early teenage years. They were supposed to accompany their older siblings or fathers to herding or hunting. In this way, they got to know how to identify areas of good pasture as well as how to deal with emergent dangers that arose during the course of herding. Warfare games were conducted during herding to prepare them for what would be their most critical task after coming of age: the defense of the community and its assets including land and livestock. Hunting game helped to show one's prowess, while at the same time hunted game meat was always an additional welcome to the family meal. Also, in their teenage years, Makonde boys were apprenticed to be good sculptors. Being a sculptor was a cherished profession among the Makonde. It took many years to refine one's skill. Among the long-distance trade-oriented communities such as the Yao, boys usually accompanied established traders on their forays into various communities while they were in their late teenage years. In this way they learned the nuances of trade: sourcing, good markets, pricing, and networking.

Women and men had their duties spelled out. People grew up knowing what their role would be in society. Indeed, this was the basis for initiating people to assume various tasks right from an early age. In traditional Mozambican societies, whether matrilineal or patrilineal, women asserted de facto powers when it came to the production of household wealth. Women farmed, traded, and accumulated wealth. The wealth a woman acquired belonged to her household and eventually went to her sons, not to the sons of her husband's wives. The husband could not arbitrarily take the wealth from one household and distribute it among other wives. He had to persuade and convince the wife to transfer wealth from one household to another. This required a lot of tact, because it could create disunity in the family.

That women headed households and accumulated wealth belies the notion that women were powerless. Contrary to what is sometimes reported in literature—that African women did not have any rights—traditional Mozambican society accorded women rights over property that they accumulated. In fact, among the matrilineal Chewa, women had a lot of power pertaining to the control of land as well as household resources. Men had fewer rights and could be dismissed and sent away by the wife.[9] The children remained with their mother. Also, egalitarianism was not the norm in most homes. Individual initiative in creating wealth was encouraged. One wife could be strong and prudent in mobilizing resources and accumulate wealth, while the converse would be true in respect to other women within the same homestead. Even in patrilineal societies, where the man was to be tactful in ensuring that one household did not suffer while others had plenty, the man had to appreciate the contribution of the hard-working wife and in so doing discourage the culture of dependency and indolence. A woman whose household experienced perpetual food shortfall was not only scorned, but became the subject of gossip.

Men controlled homesteads, which had a couple of households depending on the number of wives the person had. Besides tasks such as hunting, herding, defending the community in case of war, and leading caravans of trade, in the case of predominantly long-distance trading communities such as the Yao, men also tended to control the decision making at the homestead level. They constituted the council of elders as they grew old. The council of elders had supervisory role over lineage and clan matters. It settled disputes that could not be solved at the homestead level. It was also an important instrument through which elders ensured adherence to cultural values. They had power to warn, advise, condemn, and counsel any member of the lineage or clan that was acting outside the prescribed mores of society.

SOCIAL CHANGE

It is becoming increasingly difficult to talk about traditional African society in modern-day Mozambique. This is because a number of influences have coalesced to impact society in many and varied ways, among them Islam, Christianity, colonialism, the modern wage economy, Western education, urbanization, and emergent challenges, especially the HIV/AIDS epidemic. In some cases, the traditional cultures and customs have come under serious threat and are on the brink of being rendered irrelevant, while in other situations they have been refined to accommodate the prevailing circumstances that characterize contemporary society. Lifestyles have changed, while bonds of kinship have weakened, especially in urban areas.

The development of Western education has contributed to the erosion of the traditional informal educational system. Children attend schools run by either the government or missionaries. As a result, they spend more time in school with their peers and teachers. Parental influence is diminished. There is also less sensitivity to the culture and customs of their parents and grandparents. Instead, modern secular and missionary influences compete with the traditional values. While children who live and go to school in rural areas still show strong attachment to their rural roots, those who are born and grow up in urban areas have less attachment to the rural homesteads from where their parents hail. Furthermore, high levels of illiteracy in rural areas have worked to the disadvantage of rural teens who cannot compete with their counterparts in urban areas who have had access to modern education.

In certain cases, a teen's contribution to household chores is less than what it used to be because of education. Those who go to school in urban areas or are in boarding schools no longer tend cattle or do gardening. Their household duties are further restricted by the fact that they are in school most of the day. During their free time, those from the poor families help their parents by doing household chores. In this regard, the gender dichotomy that characterized traditional society is rather blurred. Girls and boys generally perform similar tasks. They are also exposed to modern social amenities that are unavailable in rural areas. The situation in rural households is rather different. The chores are largely unchanged: After school or on weekends the boys tend cattle while the girls still help their mothers by performing such tasks as collecting firewood or getting water from the river or well, which sometimes involve walking long distances.

The role of parents and grandparents in socializing young people and ensuring conformity with culture and customs is further diminished by the fact that children leave their homes for boarding school or high school during their formative years. Those who are successful proceed to college or urban areas in search of better opportunities in the modern economy. Teenagers in urban areas tend to be more exposed to people of various ethnic, religious, and racial persuasions. Their social network transcends their ethnic groups, and traditional customs no longer hold sway over the youth. Songs and dances in the urban areas are heavily impacted by influences from the West. Variations of African music and dances are mixed with pop sounds or jazz.

Polygyny is less prevalent today than it was in traditional society. Most Mozambicans profess faith in various religious denominations such as the Roman Catholics, Methodists, or Baptists. Total submission to traditional religion is no longer the norm. Most of the Mozambicans who have converted to the mainstream Christian denominations opt for monogamous marriage as their preferred way of marital life. They wed in churches or contract civil marriage. The situation is different in the case of Muslim converts. The Islamic faith allows for the marriage of up to four wives as long as the husband can take good care of them. But even in Islamic marriages the vows are conducted according to the Islamic faith. Traditional marriage, even though still practiced, is not accorded prominence the way it was in traditional society.

With monogamous marriages, family tends to be smaller, with fewer children, and the emphasis is on the nuclear family as opposed to the extended family. This is further encouraged by the fact that the modern economy exerts a lot of pressure on families. In the wake of scarce resources and the need to provide quality education for the children, decent housing, and healthcare, it is becoming increasingly difficult to embrace the extended family. This does not mean that those in monogamous relationships or who live in urban areas take no interest in the needs of their immediate relatives such as siblings. Nothing could be further from the truth. Most middle-income Mozambican families still strive to help their less-fortunate siblings by paying school fees, assisting in securing jobs, and, during calamities such as death, meeting burial expenses.

Kinship bonds still exist and are considered important. However, they are not reinforced the way it was done in the past. The bonds are weaker, especially among the urban elite. Also, maintaining large families is unsustainable in the wake of the modern economy with its many demands. The definition of status is changing and is no longer based on the number of wives or children one has. Wealth is no longer viewed through the prism of livestock or land per se; rather, what gives one status now is the position an individual holds in society with reference to participation in the modern economy—profession, earnings, education, investment, and the ability to lift fellow siblings by helping them gain a foothold in the modern wage sector. It is against this backdrop that most of those who are educated and have lucrative jobs are more comfortable with the modern economic and social set-up than the traditional society. The nuclear family serves them well because they have resources to meet familial needs. They engage the services of housemaids who do most of the domestic chores. There is no need to bring a relative from home to live with them to help in domestic chores. Women still have to overcome major challenges in order to gain a foothold in the modern economy. The percentage of illiterate girls is significantly higher than the percentage of illiterate boys. Girls are therefore less likely to acquire high-paying jobs. While the government is addressing this gender imbalance, it will take some time before women claim their rightful share in the Mozambican mainstream economy.

Nevertheless, Mozambican women are hard working and contribute significantly to the economy. In the rural areas, they head and sustain households in cases where the husband has gone to the town for wage labor. Men who work in the cities usually send money to their wives to help supplement the household income. An important outcrop of this change is the fact that men in urban areas perform tasks that they would not otherwise do in the presence of their wives. They wash their own clothes and cook and serve their meal themselves. In the rural areas, the women take on both paternal and maternal roles. This has blurred the age and gender basis of the labor organizations that characterized traditional society.

One significant manifestation of the impact of modern economy on gender work relations is the increase in the number of women who work in the mainstream economy.[10] They work in food processing and textile factories. There are also professional and career women who are highly placed in the public and nascent private sector. They are in the teaching and health professions as well. Even in the realm of politics, women have been active in the Frelimo movement. Female domesticity is no longer in vogue. While it is true that women are still predominantly in the nonformal sector of the economy, especially in retail businesses, their empowerment as a result of the modern economy is not insignificant.

Migration to the cities has brought with it a number of new developments that threaten the moral fabric of traditional societies. The migration to urban centers has been on the rise in the last couple of decades. Urban areas are associated with job opportunities, which in most cases are not sufficient to cope with the number of unemployed. In the wake of joblessness, women and men find it hard to survive. They are forced to resort to petty trade, which includes selling used clothing as well as fruits and foodstuffs. Some of the migrants to the towns are teenagers who have just completed primary or high school. In the absence of the traditional family, especially a father and mother who are symbols of authority, these young people become quite vulnerable to the temptations of high life in urban areas. City life emanates individualism and anonymity, as in daily life many contacts are made between children and other members of society; but none of these contacts are meaningful enough to generate true social capital. The traditional society, through its tightly controlled educational system, kinship structure, and familial support initiatives, minimized the problem of destitution by providing economic, social, and emotional security.

Vulnerable teenagers who cannot rely on their extended family, as is traditional, or on other members of society for help will often turn to a peer group to gain social capital in an attempt to meet their needs. They may get involved in premarital sexual relations, and children are born out of wedlock to teenage mothers who are sometimes unprepared for the challenges of motherhood. When vulnerable children are confronted with difficult circumstances, as they often are in urban settings, they can no longer rely on their extended family safety nets to protect them. When children slip through these safety nets in the urban setting, they often will become street children to try and satisfy their needs. The problem of abandoned and street children constitutes a challenge for the Mozambican government and society. These problems are further compounded by the onset of HIV/AIDS that has devastated families, albeit comparatively less than the current situation in some of the southern African countries.

Thousands of children are left orphans not only in the urban areas, but in the rural ones as well. Since life expectancy remains low at 40.2 years for women and 38.4 for men,[11] the care giving and nurturing of children are undergoing fundamental change. Because parents die young, grandparents are now parenting children across the country. In turn, children are beginning to assume roles that were hitherto monopolized by their parents. It is not uncommon to find children in their early teens taking care of their younger siblings as well as parents who are unable to fend for themselves and the children because they are immobilized by HIV/AIDS. With the present HIV/AIDS prevalence rate of 13.6 percent the situation is overwhelming, taking into account the fact that close to 70 percent of the population lives at or below the absolute poverty level.[12]

Nongovernmental organizations (NGOs) funded by charitable organizations and international organizations such as USAID and UNAIDS are playing vital roles in mobilizing the youth and raising awareness toward containing the spread of HIV/AIDS. As a result, terms such as condoms, abstinence, testing, and counseling are in the public domain. Billboards are used to convey the message to Mozambicans, young, middle-aged, and old. Churches too have HIV/AIDS outreach programs aimed at educating the faithful. The open discussion of sex among members of different generations that was a taboo in traditional society is now a matter of public discourse in local meetings spearheaded by health officials, church leaders, NGOs, and politicians. Individuals, lineages, clans, communities, and their customs and cultures are being interrogated as society goes through the difficult and trying period of balancing tradition and the persistent reality of deaths, orphans, and destitution.

Despite the foregoing changes that characterize Mozambican society, there are certain core values that are still cherished by segments of the population regardless of their educational, religious, and economic status. The payment of bride wealth, lobola, is considered critical to the consummation of any marriage. Thus those who opt for Christian or civil marriage still pay or receive lobola. The amount involved has gone up, especially for girls who have attained higher education and earn decent wages. The situation is hardly any different for converts to Islam. In Islamic marriages, the ceremony implies a contract between individuals, but little change in the system of alliance between two families. Almsgiving, sadaq, is incorporated into the bride wealth guarantee.[13] Furthermore, respect for old people is still honored by most Mozambican communities. Disrespecting an elder is considered rude and evokes rebuke and condemnation.

But all in all, it has to be emphasized that the traditional multilayered system is giving way to a nuclear family oriented system, with its inherent strengths and weaknesses. The rise in the number of single mothers as well as female-headed households, single men, and children born out of wedlock are signs that the traditional society and its prescribed mores are no longer esteemed. Also, modern developments ranging from education and religion to economy and urbanization are providing alternatives that were at best minimal in traditional society. The onset of the HIV/AIDS epidemic is forcing Mozambican communities to interrogate their customs and cultures. Indeed, no society holds onto a tradition if it leads to its death. It is therefore not surprising to notice the many changes that Mozambican society has embraced and continues to incorporate in order to ensure and guarantee its survival for the good of its members.

NOTES

1. For a history of the Yao, especially their involvement in long-distance commerce, see Edward A. Alpers, *Ivory and Slaves in East Central Africa: Changing Patterns of International Trade to the Later Nineteenth Century* (London: Heinemann, 1975).

2. John Stoner, *Makonde* (New York: Rosen Publishing Group, 1998), 31–32.

3. John S. Mbiti, *Love and Marriage in Africa* (London: Longman Group Limited, 1973), 90–97.

4. Stoner, *Makonde,* 29.

5. Allen F. Isaacman and Barbara S. Isaacman, *Slavery and Beyond: The Making of Men and Chikunda Ethnic Identities in the Unstable World of South-Central Africa, 1750–1920* (London: Heinemann, 2004); Eric J. Hobsbawn and Terence Ranger, eds., *The Invention of Tradition* (Cambridge: Cambridge University Press, 1992).

6. Stoner, *Makonde.*

7. Harold K. Schneider, *The Africans: An Ethnological Account* (Upper Saddle River, NJ: Prentice-Hall, 1981), 91–92.

8. Diane Kayongo-Male and Philista Onyango, *The Sociology of the African Family* (New York: Longman Group, 1984), 13.

9. Schneider, *The Africans,* 91.

10. Stephanie Urdang, *And Still They Dance: Women, War, and the Struggle for Change in Mozambique* (New York: Monthly Review Press, 1989), 152–170.

11. http://www.usaid.gov/locations/sub-Saharan_Africa/countries/Mozambique.

12. http://www.usaid.gov/locations/sub-Saharan_Africa/countries/Mozambique.

13. J. Spencer Trimingham, *The Influence of Islam upon Africa* (London and New York: Longman, 1980), 51.

7

Social Customs and Lifestyle

SOCIAL RELATIONS

MOZAMBICANS CHERISH interpersonal relations because of the nature of familial and communal relationships that characterize society. Extended family is the norm, especially in the rural areas. Relationships are defined in terms of son, daughter, father, mother, grandparents, uncles and aunts, both maternal and paternal, and in-laws.[1] How to interact with the various relatives necessitated a code of behavior that has been institutionalized by the society. The code of behavior defines everything from greetings, consultation, advice, and counseling to the receiving and giving of gifts. There is sensitivity to age, gender, wealth, power, and seniority in lineage. The emphasis is on respect and humility. The two are considered the pillars that ensure harmony and peace among individuals for the benefit of the wider community. Indeed, children are taught the code of behavior in order to make them responsible members of the family, community, and society when they come of age. Even in urban areas where the nuclear family is taking hold at a fast rate, the code of behavior is often evident when those who live in urban areas visit with their relatives in the rural areas. Cosmopolitanism does not free one from the bonds and obligations of interpersonal relationships.

Greeting is considered an important aspect of interpersonal relations. Shaking hands during greeting is deeply appreciated. It is considered not only a show of warmth and respect, but also a way of connecting with one in a special way. Individuals of the same age or generation usually get involved in a hearty handshake, especially if they have not seen one another for a long time. During handshaking the individuals will be chatting and exchanging kind words.

The situation is different if one is greeting an elder or person of one's father's generation. In such circumstances, the younger person is not supposed to maintain eye contact with the elder person. Direct eye contact with an elder is considered a sign of disrespect. This is contrary to the situation in the West, where eye contact is considered very important as a way of connecting with the other person. In Mozambican societies, the younger person is expected to extend his hand and bow as he greets an elderly person. Also, the greeting is rather short and not as elaborate as that between individuals of the same age group. An elaborate handshake with a person of the opposite sex is discouraged unless he/she is an acquaintance. It is considered bad manners and could easily lead to uneasiness on the part of the other party, especially the female.

If individuals are not in close enough proximity to shake hands, they are still expected to greet one another either by waving or by just exchanging words of greeting. In the rural setting, one can greet many people in the course of a day. Indeed, the first thing within the homestead one does upon waking up is to greet everyone and ask how they are doing or how their morning is. When greeted one must respond in acknowledgement. There is a common saying among most communities in Mozambique that greeting is free. As a result, it is considered rude and evil not to greet. Even strangers deserve to be greeted. Mozambicans are very courteous and would go out of their way to show you directions to a place if you are lost. In a sense, greeting is an important way of establishing a rapport with a stranger to determine if she/he needs help, especially in the rural areas. One can seek direction to a place by greeting a person and asking to be shown a place.

The situation is different in urban settings. Shaking hands during greeting is less common. People are contented with exchanging words of greeting rather than handshaking, because people tend to be busy and have less time for elaborate greetings. The setting itself is not conducive to elaborate shaking of hands, as this interferes with movement of people on the streets. Also, interactions with people who are not acquaintances and relatives tend to be more formal and solemn. Nevertheless, Mozambicans still maintain the tradition of shaking hands during greeting if they know the individual well or he/she is from their home region. However, young people growing up in urban areas are less concerned with the niceties of shaking hands. A simple gesture of acknowledgement of another's presence sometimes just suffices.

Since age is important, the elderly are accorded due respect across the ethnic divide. The respect tends to vary based on the position held by the individual elder in society. If an elder has accumulated a lot of wealth he will be more respected than one who is not well endowed. Similarly, an elder who holds a position of seniority in the village will be accorded due respect by his fellow elders as well as by members of the younger generation. Combining the two, age and wealth, is an asset. This is because such accumulation of wealth was once used to sustain a large family and host beer parties at which the elder would be praised and his generosity applauded. But perhaps most important is the fact that Mozambican communities associate age with wisdom. Generally, it is considered impolite to argue with or answer back an elder. Such behavior stands condemned.

The elders are the custodians of societal values and their word on customary practices is considered final. Thus it is not uncommon to find relatives who live far away traveling long distance to report an incident to the patriarch of the family for informational purposes or to seek his indulgence in solving a dispute. The elder is supposed to be diligent, forthright, fair, and balanced in settling any dispute so that his verdict is beyond reproach. On the basis of his authority and power as the patriarch of the family the verdict delivered is supposed to be respected by all. The patriarch, as is indeed the case with most elders, is considered a major depository of communal knowledge and expertise. Any challenge to that authority and power could evoke the wrath and curse of the patriarch. Such a curse is believed to bring misfortune to an individual and his/her family.

Because of the nature of the extended family, visiting relatives is considered part of growing up as a member of the community. This is important because the young gets to know the relatives who do not live with them in the homestead and/or region. Visiting aunts, uncles, and cousins provides the individual with the opportunity to explore life outside the immediate family, get to know other places, socialize, and strengthen family bond and interpersonal relationships. A visiting relative is treated as a member of the family and is not supposed to get any special treatment. He/she is considered a member of the homestead. The obligations and responsibilities remain unchanged from the place of origin.

Interpersonal relations are also reflected in the way various members of a family or clans who live in close proximity help one another in undertaking certain chores. Members of the extended family usually offer a helping hand during planting, weeding, or harvesting as well as myriad other chores. In certain demanding situations, members come together to offer such services to an individual to ease his/her burden. They are not paid in cash. Instead, the host prepares food and beer that the visiting family members partake of after completing the chores. In this way members of the extended family help their own. Such communal labor helps a family cope with a shortage of labor during peak seasons of plowing, planting, weeding, and harvesting. Interestingly, it is expected that a member of the family who has a bumper harvest will help the less fortunate members by giving or loaning them grain to help alleviate famine. This arrangement ensures that the family, clan, or community takes care of their own by helping one another. In a sense, this economy of affection enhances interpersonal relations.

Gift giving is very much appreciated. It is courteous to take gifts to relatives when visiting. Gifts can take many forms: grain, chicken, or other groceries such as sugar and cooking oil. It is not the amount that matters; rather, it is the spirit of giving. Similarly, visiting relatives do not return to their homes empty-handed. They are given gifts to take back with them. Reciprocity of gifts is an important aspect of interpersonal relations. During hard times such as drought, famine, or floods in one part of the country, relatives who live in places that are unaffected usually help those extended family members who are economically stressed and need assistance. In the same vein, it is prudent to take a gift to one's relatives when visiting, especially if they live in the rural areas and are less endowed. Such gifts are very much appreciated, and one who gives is usually the subject of praise by the local relatives.

CEREMONIES

Ceremonies associated with birth, initiation, marriage, and death help to give distinctiveness, uniqueness, and cultural identity to various rites of passage that are considered integral to individuals' initiation into and acceptance by the community. Ceremonies bring people together as witnesses to appreciate their rich cultural heritage by creating transcendental meaning of their relationships and existence as a community. Rites of passage that usually involve elaborate ceremonies include birth, initiation to adulthood, marriage, and death. Each right of passage is considered unique because it constitutes a defining episode in the life of the individual as one journeys through life. It is a mark of aging and gaining experience through the many stages of life. The attendant ceremonies are characterized by actions and activities that range from singing and dancing to seclusion and education.

Birth

The birth of a child brings joy and pride to the couple, family, and clan. However, the joyous occasion is sometimes not so cherished if the child is born under peculiar conditions such as the death of a twin, or a newborn with some defect, or as a result of a feet-first birth. Such peculiarities signal a bad omen and are usually dealt with by involving a diviner or medicine man. If the birth is normal the child is welcomed with pomp, and there is great feasting. The mother is taken good care of by being given food and drinks to restore her health. Her aunts and co-wives are always there to nurse and ensure that she is comfortable. Breastfeeding is the accepted and preferred way of nurturing the newborn. Naming usually takes place immediately after birth or shortly thereafter.

Initiation

The second most important rite of passage is that of initiation into adulthood. Girls and boys are initiated differently. Initiation of girls, *cipitu,* among the Makonde emphasizes hard work, obedience, and responsible womanhood.[2] Girls go through cipitu when they are 10 to 12 years old. It is village based, and therefore it is the head of the village who determines when the time is ready for initiation. The head of the village, invariably a man, chooses a female elder to lead the process by being the chief instructor of the initiates as they go through the process. Girls are secluded in a special house set aside for the purpose of housing the initiates during the initiation period. During this period the girls are taught how to be good mothers, the meaning and significance of sex in marriage, and their role as wives and mothers in society.

In spite of the solemnity that characterizes the instructions during the process, initiation is also a time of joy and happiness as evidenced by the singing, drumming, and dancing that grace the festivity. Villagers join the initiates in celebrating their newly acquired status as initiates into the society. On their graduation and subsequent release from seclusion, the girls are anointed with oil and dressed in new clothes. This symbolizes that they are entering a new period of life. As honored members of the community, they are privileged to watch the *mudimu* dance that is performed by women to welcome them back into the society after their days in seclusion.[3] As they come of age and get ready for marriage, the initiates work with their mothers, grandmothers, and older female members of their families to be prepared for the challenges of motherhood that they will face in the not too distant future.

In contrast, the initiation of boys, *jando,* is more formal, elaborate, and takes much longer.[4] It is less frequently undertaken than the girl's ceremony because of the cost and time constraints that are involved in preparing jando. The ceremony involves boys aged between 10 and 16. Many villages, each of which produces the boys for initiation, attend the ceremony. The initiates are housed in a shelter, *likumbi,* which is specially built by the village for this important ceremony. It is in the likumbi where educational instructions pertaining to the societal way of life are inculcated into the initiates. Adherence to the basic tenets of societal life such as respect, discipline, obedience, hard work, and endurance is emphasized. It is these tenets that guarantee success in society. Songs, stories, and sayings are used to impart the knowledge.

The initiation process is headed and patronized over by a spiritual specialist, a *mkukomela.* His attire and persona reflects the solemnity of his task.

He carries a basket of sacred medicines and a whisk made from the tail of a wildebeest and wear charms on his upper arm. Mkukomela is assisted by a *mnombo,* or godfather, who is supposed to encourage the initiate to go through the process. Sacred flour is rubbed on the initiates' foreheads on the day of the circumcision, after which they are taken out of the likumbi to the countryside where the physical operation of circumcision is conducted.

Among the Makua, it is the elder of the clan, *Mwene,* who presides over the initiation ceremony.[5] *Namku,* the equivalent of the Makonde's *mnobo,* assists him. Namku takes on the day-to-day care of the initiates during the initiation period, including the three weeks after the physical act, when the wound is supposed to heal. The physical act is important because in all the communities that practice circumcision it is impossible to get married without going through the act, because you are considered immature for not having graduated to adulthood and been taught about the responsibilities of marital life. It is important to note that the physical act is the last episode in this elaborate ceremony because it crowns the instructions that precede it and is considered significant in the development from childhood to adulthood. After the ceremony the initiates return to their respective villages and assume new names and dress in new clothes symbolizing the dawn of a new era of adulthood and a complete break with the preceding stage of childhood.

Ceremonies pertaining to African circumcision are thus significant because they not only help the initiates to understand and appreciate historical information pertaining to their cultural group and rituals, but they also fulfill the vital function of forging a cultural and collective identity as a people. In addition, such initiation crowns the educational process that helps initiates to understand the meaning and significance of social control, sexual identity, and individual responsibility. These initiatives help to reinforce the prevailing norms of gender and appropriate behavior. It is not surprising therefore that no Makua girl would expect to get married before going through the initiation ceremony called *Matengusi,* which takes place after the girl attains puberty. *Matengusi* does not involve circumcision, but education and training pertaining to motherhood and attendant responsibilities.[6]

In contrast to the foregoing elaborate circumcision rites, Muslims differ in the way they view the ritual of initiation. Among the Moslems who live in coastal communities as well as in the urban centers in the hinterland, initiation is seen as an individual rite, a ceremony of purification.

The traditional societies see initiation both as a social rite and as a vital ceremony that represents the collective will of the community for the specific purposes of marking the transition from one stage of life to the next as well as a means of instructing the initiates into the community's traditions and customs.

Marriage

Marriage is equally important as a rite among Mozambican communities. It takes place after the two individuals have gone through the rites of passage, which qualifies them as adults who understand the meaning and seriousness of marriage with all its attendant responsibilities. Arranged marriages are not uncommon, but the bride and groom usually get to know one another before marriage. Sex was traditionally understood as a means of exploring, strengthening, deepening, and cementing the relationship that came with marriage. As a result, premarital sex was discouraged. That is not necessarily the case these days, when premarital sex is more frequent. Marriage is solemnized through the payment of bride wealth, lobola. Upon payment of lobola, the bride moves to the groom's home in patriarchal societies, while in matrilineal societies the groom moves to the bride's home and settles among his wife's people. Marriage brings joy not only to the married couple, but also to their families. It is a bond that unites the couple, the families, and societies.

However, not all marriages follow the foregoing traditional pattern. This is because marriage across ethnic lines is now more widespread than ever before because of mobility brought on by modern education as well as wage labor. There is emerging an urban population that identifies with the city. Their ways tend to be cosmopolitan and therefore less prone to traditional and/or rural customs. Thus, there are couples who opt for Christian ceremonies. In such cases, Christian rites apply, and they go through the specific church pastoral programs for education and advice pertaining to marriage. A wedding is subsequently arranged after consulting with both families. The marriage is subsequently solemnized in church, where the bride and groom exchange vows and sign the marriage certificate.

Among the Muslims, marriage is based on written law and is primarily a contract between two fathers. Also, there is a major distinction between Islamic and traditional African marriages because the former allows marriage among relatives, especially cousins. This was a taboo and was totally unacceptable in the case of African traditional marriages. Indeed, even Christianity prohibits such marriages. Before formal engagement the family of the groom consults a diviner to ensure that the marriage will be successful and graced with children. If the marriage will be successful, the groom's family approaches the girl's parents and offers a gift, *utashi* or *kosa,* before transmitting a proposal.[7] If the proposal is accepted and discussion pertaining to bride wealth is concluded, contract money, *mahari,* must be paid for the bride as well as in two essential payments to the parents. The two are *kilemba,* turban money to the father, and *mkaja* or *mweleko* to the mother. Following the payment of bride wealth and the essential gifts due to the father and mother of the bride, the contract ceremony takes place at the mosque, court, or house in the presence of the presiding cleric as well as witnesses and the father or guardian of the girl. Upon accepting the vows, the cleric declares the couple husband and wife. The wedding feast follows this solemnization of the ceremony.

Traditionally, public display of love such as kissing or holding hands in public was discouraged. There is an element of conservatism that pervades most African societies when it comes to public display of love. Islam also exhibits similar conservatism and is even stricter when it comes to exposure of the female body. Muslim women who strictly adhere to Islamic values always veil themselves. This does not mean that couples do not show love to one another. Nothing could be further from the truth. Songs as well as poetry expressing deep affection for a partner are commonplace. There is deep appreciation for the spouse. The only problem is touching a partner in public in a show of intimacy. Married couples are supposed to be role models for the young people. Kissing in public or holding of hands was viewed as sending a bad example to the young people, which is considered bad manners and is generally unacceptable. Good conduct and moral behavior dictate that adults show little public emotion on issues pertaining to love and sex. The situation is changing in the wake of exposure to Western media, movies, and music. For the young generation the old taboos are now acceptable. Nevertheless, most men would be hesitant in kissing their girlfriends in public when visiting rural areas that still tend to be conservative. Similarly, such public displays of love would invite rebuke from parents or relatives in urban areas if they still hold dear their traditional values.

Death

The final episode in one's life is death. In death, the individual is subject to a rite of passage in which he/she retreats forever from the space of the living. It brings sorrow and sadness to the deceased's family and clan. Death is unwanted. Bad spirits are believed to cause death. The Makua, as indeed all communities in the country, believe that we lose our lives and die because of very strong evil forces that are beyond human control. Fellow human beings through witchcraft can also cause death. The common denominator is that for a death there must be an induced cause either by evil forces or witchcraft. As a result, it is not uncommon to find a person fingered for being responsible for causing the death of the deceased. A witch or a person who is believed to have had a grudge with the deceased and supposedly contributed to the individual's death stands condemned. There is no belief in death due to natural causes.

All communities in Mozambique attach great significance to the mourning and subsequent disposal of the body of the deceased. While the death of every individual is regretted regardless of age, gender, and wealth, the accompanying ceremonies differ based on those variables. A child's loss is painful. However, it involves less elaborate ceremonies than those of an adult. Among the Makua the clan elder, *Mwene,* is informed immediately when a person is pronounced dead.[8] The Mwene conveys the clan's condolences to the widow/widower of the deceased by handing over a black fowl or cock, depending on the gender of the deceased, to the surviving spouse. If the deceased is a woman the fowl is presented and if it is a man the cock is given to the widow. The blackness signifies sadness, sorrow, and calamity. In consultation with the family elders, the Mwene also releases burial arrangements. If the Mwene dies, the other elders, *Mamwene,* will consult widely and assume responsibility in conducting the funerary rites pertaining to the deceased Mwene.

Death leads to the suspension of all other nonfuneral duties in the village. Life returns to normal after the third day in a ceremony called *Nihuku nowshinga.* On the third day members of the deceased's family have their hair shaved, and the deceased's surviving spouse(s) are allowed to stroll outside of the home adorned in black attire symbolizing their state of loss. The ceremony is attended by many people who could number into the hundreds depending on the name, recognition, and esteem of the deceased. Nihuku nowishinga marks the official end of the mourning period, after which life is supposed to return to normal, albeit not necessarily for the immediate family members of the deceased. Thus while death has the painful distinction of being a rite of passage defined by brutal finality, the departed has the will to live behind good or bad memories. Based on one's conduct in this life, the deceased is assured of good or bad memories after his departure from this world.

In the context of those who profess Islamic faith, Islamic law strictly guides death and attendant funerary rights. A cleric is usually summoned to recite chapters from the Quran and offer prayers when a faithful is near the point of death. This is very similar to Christianity, especially Roman Catholics, when priests are summoned during such situations to anoint a seriously or terminally ill person. The purpose of reciting chapters from Quran and offering prayers is to prepare the soul as it prepares to depart. There are four rituals surrounding death: the washing of the dead, *kuosha maiti;* the burial, *maziko;* funeral, *matanga;* and closure of the mourning period after 40 days, *arbaini.*[9] The deceased's body is put on a mat after being washed. The mat is then put on a bier and covered with cloth of honor. All the materials used—mat, cloth, and bier—are fumigated. The body is then carried to the grave as the faithful recite verses and prayers. During maziko the body is laid to rest and the grave is filled. This is then followed by the mourn-ing period, matanga, which generally lasts three days. Relatives live under the same roof as they share their grief. They receive mourners who come to console them. Quran verses are recited. Even though normal activities resume after the third day, the mourning period is supposed to continue for the next 40 days. The grave is visited on the fortieth day, during which time prayers are offered and people feast. The soul is believed to depart shortly after that.

TRADITIONAL AND MODERN NATIONAL AND RELIGIOUS DAYS

Religious Days

There are three major religions in Mozambique. These include indige-nous faiths (50 percent), Christianity (30 percent), and Islam (20 percent). Each of these religions has religious days that are usually observed. The main Christian religious days are Easter and Christmas. Easter is the commemora-tion of the death and subsequent resurrection of Jesus Christ. It does not have a fixed day, but it is usually celebrated in early April. The holy weekend that commemorates the event is marked by prayer and kicks off on Good Friday. On this day, Christians reflect on the mystery of the cross, especially its sym-bolic embodiment of Jesus Christ's suffering and death. They are called upon to reflect on the ultimate sacrifice that Jesus Christ made in order to save mankind. The high point of the Easter weekend is Sunday, which is the main day of prayer. The faithful go to church where the priests/pastors lead the faithful in a number of masses. The resurrection gives Christians hope that there is life beyond the present life. By emphasizing the resurrection of Jesus and his triumph over death, Christians emphasize the immortality of the soul and their continued life in the hereafter where they will meet their creator and share in his glory.

The other Christian religious day is Christmas, which celebrates the birth of Jesus Christ. It takes place on December 25. Christians throng to churches on December 24 at midnight. Those who live far from the church travel long distances to spend the night celebrating the midnight mass. More masses are said the next day. Depending on the size of the congregation, as many as five or six masses may be conducted by various priests/pastors. Christmas is not only about religious activities. It has come to include extra-religious activities that include heavy shopping, feasting, and gift giving. For retail traders, both in the major cities and in rural trading centers, Christmas is one of the seasons when they experience brisk business. People host parties and eat and drink to their fill. Those in towns usually travel to their rural homes to share the day with their families, because government offices are closed on Christmas day and workers are given the day off. Thus, while Christmas is primarily a religious holiday, its effect transcends the religious sphere and impacts business as well as leisure activities.

Muslims also have various festivals as well as religious days that are observed regularly, the two most important of which are *Ramadan* and *Eid-el-Fitr*. In the holy month of Ramadan, Muslims fast for 30 days, from sunrise to sunset. They abstain from sex, food, and drink during the day. Ramadan takes place some time in March or April, beginning when the full moon appears. As a result, the beginning and end of Ramadan are still determined empirically and vary from one region to the next based on the sighting of the moon. Ramadan as a month of fasting and mortification is a period of religious renewal. Fasting strengthens believers' voices so that Allah may hear them. It is seen as the gateway to divine service. Fasting during Ramadan is one of the pillars of Islam. After sunset, the faithful gather in mosques where they reflect on the solemn religiosity of the day. After the prayer gathering, the faithful eat their meal for the next 24 hours. During Ramadan there is an abundance of charity as well as increased attendance at mosques. Eid-el-Fitr marks the end of the month of Ramadan. It is a day of great celebration characterized by singing, feasting, and displays of grandeur and generosity.

Besides Ramadan and Eide-el-Fitr, the other important festivals are *Eid-el-Kabir* and *Eid-el-Maulud*. The former is held for two days to commemorate the end of the hajj, which is the pilgrimage to the holy city of Mecca that a devout Muslim is supposed to undertake. Not only prayer, but also feasting and entertainment that include children's plays, music, and dance conclude Eid-El-Kabir. Eid-el-Maulud, which is celebrated in September, marks the birthday of the Prophet Muhammad. Both holidays are characterized by a mixture of prayer, generosity, and feasting.

National Holidays

Mozambique also celebrates national days that are not associated with any religion. Indeed, during the early days of independence from Portugal, the Frelimo government steered the country toward a socialist path that had no place for religious holidays. This was a reversal from the situation during the colonial days when Christian religious days were treated as national holidays with offices and businesses closed. However, even though the Frelimo government did not recognize the days by giving workers off, most faithful still adhered to those religious days in the privacy of their homes, communities, and churches or mosques.

The nonreligious days include New Year's Day (January 1), Mozambican Heroes' Day (February 3), Mozambican Women's Day (April 7), Workers' Day (May 1), Independence Day (June 25), Armed Forces' Day (September 25), and Family Day (December 25). During these national days, government offices as well as businesses are closed and workers are given time off. Independence Day commemorates the day when the country attained its independence from Portugal, while on Workers' Day Mozambicans reflect on the contribution of the workers to the building of the country. In the early years of Frelimo rule, Workers' Day was arguably one of the most significant days because the government asserted that it was constructing a worker's state. This meant that the workers constituted the very foundation of the republic.

Heroes' Day is significant because it commemorates the struggles by Mozambicans to liberate the country from Portuguese colonial rule. It is a reminder of the sacrifice of the freedom fighters, many of whom were either maimed or died in the cause of freedom struggle. Many more lost their property and were displaced as the freedom struggle raged on for nearly two decades. Like Independence Day, Heroes' Day is celebrated with pomp and pageantry as evidenced in the displays by the military as a show of resolve and strength to defend the country's territorial integrity. The high point of the celebrations is the presidential address, which applauds the sacrifices made by the country's heroes. Heroes' Day is very similar in meaning with Armed Forces' Day, which commemorates the fallen as well as serving members of the armed forces for their bravery and courage in fighting wars, both within and outside of the country.

New Year's Day is celebrated almost worldwide when people usher in the New Year. Just like Family Day, New Year's Day provides families with the opportunity to rejoice together. There is feasting, sports, and music. Those in urban areas go to clubs to celebrate with their friends. Women's Day is one of the most significant holidays in Mozambique because of women's role in various sectors of life: economy, politics, and the liberation struggle. Mozambican women were pivotal in the liberation struggle as fighters, suppliers of food and military hardware to the fighters, and in sustaining the households during the struggle. The day is not only a reminder of the many accomplishments of women in the past couple of decades, but also of the myriad challenges that they still face in overcoming poverty and gaining access to education and healthcare.

LEISURE

Amusement and Sports

Mozambique offers many entertainment activities. The country has some of the most beautiful beaches in the world. Mozambicans frequent the beaches during national days when they have time off from their places of work. Also, tourists from as close as South Africa and as far as Europe visit the Mozambican coast every year to enjoy its sandy beaches. Off the Mozambican coast is a group of islands that are equally frequented because of fine beaches and clear water where tourists can swim and sunbathe as they watch flamingos and dolphins.

The presence of national parks provides Mozambicans as well as visitors the opportunity to view wildlife. Fortunately, most of the parks are located in close proximity to the major cities. The Gorongosa Game Reserve, which is located north of Beira, attracts thousands of visitors every year because of its buffaloes, lions, elephants, and hippos. Similarly, Maputo National Park, which is located south of the capital, is home to herds of elephants. Thus, visiting one of the two major cities one can spend leisure time venturing into the parks to see what Mozambique provides in terms of its wildlife.

Among youths, music provides the best form of entertainment. Mozambique boasts cafes, bars, and clubs throughout the country. Youths frequents these places, especially during weekends and national days. Music either from a jukebox or local bands offering live concerts entertains the patrons. Besides music, there is beer drinking and food. Some patrons enjoy the company of their friends, while those who are unaccompanied may request a dance from single patrons. Besides the music and beer, the occasion provides the youth with the opportunity to meet new friends or to relax and chat with other patrons after a hard day's work. Some Mozambicans like to relax within the privacy of their homes, where they watch popular television programs and share their time with family members.

In the rural areas where television is unavailable, young people spend time with their parents or grandparents listening to stories that extol societal values such as morality, courage, respect, and hard work. Rural teens engage in craftsmanship such as woodcarving, through which they are apprenticed to the trade. While this is part of training to be a professional, it is not uncommon to find rural teens spend their leisure time watching and/or participating in the making of some artwork.

Hunting is another important leisure activity undertaken by both young and middle-aged men in the countryside. Also, during herding, bullfighting is commonplace. The herders identify and cheer bulls on to fight as a form of entertainment.

Mozambicans cherish and participate in a variety of sports. The most popular is soccer, which is also a form of recreation. In schools, towns, and rural markets, National League Soccer commands a massive following. Institutions of learning from primary through university organize soccer competitions where the winners are rewarded with trophies. National and international soccer matches draw thousands of funs. Those whose team wins celebrate, while the losers go home heartbroken. International matches between

Mozambique and other countries, whether played within or outside of the country, captivate the nation, with thousands glued to the television if the match is broadcast live. Many more listen to the radio. During such international soccer competitions, Mozambicans are totally unified in support of their team. The national team participates in the regional soccer tournament as well as in continental cup tournaments, the African Cup of Nations, and World Cup qualifying matches.

Besides soccer, Mozambicans also remain great fans of track events. The country has some of the best runners. One of the country's most renowned athletes is Maria Mutola, whose initial interest was in soccer. She played and competed with boys. At age 18, she turned to running and became the first Mozambican to win the Olympic gold for her country, competing in the 800-meter race during the 1996 games held in Atlanta, Georgia. Maria Mutola has been a source of inspiration to the youth of Mozambique. In recognition of her accomplishment she was accorded special honor by then-President Chissano of Mozambique. Other sports that are popular in Mozambique include netball, volleyball, boxing, wrestling, and field hockey. Netball is primarily a women's sport. Both men and women play volleyball. Boxing and wrestling are predominantly men's sports. In sum, however, these sports do not command the massive following that soccer and running have in the country.

Cinema

Cinema is not only a modern source of leisure; it also plays a vital role in promoting policies that impact people's lives. One of the first cultural acts of the Frelimo government after independence was to establish the National Institute of Cinema (INC), primarily for political reasons. It was to be used in mobilizing the people to support the socialist cause of the Frelimo platform by making and showing films that cast the government in a positive light. Indeed, one of most celebrated films, *Samora Machel: Son of Africa,* is based on an exclusive interview that the founding president gave to a filmmaker. It shows Machel as one of the most important freedom fighters and revolutionaries that helped shape the destiny of Mozambique.

Cinema is used as an effective tool in the fight against HIV/AIDS. FilmAfrik is an initiative sponsored by a Maputo-based production company called Iris Imaginacoes that focuses on bringing African films to African audiences in African communities. It has been instrumental in showing films in various parts of the country, including rural areas. One such film is the Portuguese version of *The Yellow Card*, the movie *Cartao Amarelo*. Its nationwide distribution was partly funded by Pathfinder International of Mozambique.

Cinemoval Group is another important organization that has as its primary focus the use of film to convey the message of change when it comes to matters pertaining to HIV/AIDS and other development challenges. Through such groups, a storyline is narrated in such a way that it provokes people to think about their plight. Subjects that were hitherto considered taboos in discussions pertaining to sex are demystified and discussed openly, thereby saving lives.

As a form of entertainment, cinemas are found in practically all the major towns in Mozambique. In Maputo there are many theaters where one can go and watch a movie. These include the Xenon, Gil Vicente, and Scala cinemas. They show different films at any one given time. There are billboards outside the cinema that indicates the film being shown. Listings of current and coming films are also available in the local dailies. Depending on the movie shown, the cinemas are invariably full during the weekends. They are also heavily frequented in the evenings during the workweek.

Television is equally popular, especially in areas where the reception is good. Because television programs offer a variety of films, plays, and other forms of entertainment such as music and soccer, cinema faces stiff competition. However, many people cherish cinema because some of the productions are local and people can identify with the characters, scenes, and message. The clash of cultures is also an important theme that is very popular and usually draws many fans to the theaters.

In sum, societies in Mozambique are dynamic and constantly embrace the changes that are consistent with modern trends. Western education, increased urbanization, Christianity, media, and politics all combine to impact the way Mozambicans relate to one another as well as to those from outside of their communities. In the process, traditional customs that are deemed to be out of step with the modern realities are discarded. Similarly, those customs that are important to society are reinvigorated to better serve the society. Social customs and lifestyles in Mozambique are a reflection of the interplay of tradition and the forces of change through time.

NOTES

1. Diane Kayongo-Male and Philista Onyango, *The Sociology of the African Family* (London and New York: Longman, 1984), 1–11; Toyin Falola, "Intergroup Relations," in Toyin Falola, ed., *Africa Volume 2: African Cultures and Societies before 1885* (Durham, NC: Carolina Academic Press, 2000), 19; Austin M. Ahanotu, "Social Institutions: Kinship Systems," in Toyin Falola, ed., *Africa Volume 2,* 35–42.

2. John Stoner, *Makonde* (New York: Rosen Publishing Group, 1998), 30.

3. John Stoner, *Makonde,* 30–31.

4. John Stoner, *Makonde,* 28–30. Also see Max Mohl, *Masterpieces of the Makonde* (Heidelberg: Max Mohl, 1989).

5. Kazimierz Kubat and Edwin Mpokasaye, "Excerpts of Makua Traditions" [web article], http://www.sds-ch.ch/centre/artyk/articel/makua.htm. Cited February 26, 2006.

6. Kubat and Mpokasaye, "Excerpts."

7. J. Spencer Trimingham, *The Influence of Islam upon Africa* (London and New York: Longman, 1980), 53–84. Edward A. Alpers, "East Central Africa," in Nehemia Levtzion and Randall L. Pouwels, eds., *The History of Islam in Africa* (Athens: Ohio University Press, 2000), 303–326.

8. Kubat and Mpokasaye, "Excerpts."

9. J. Spencer Trimingham, *Islam in East Africa* (Oxford, UK: Clarendon Press, 1964), 140–141.

8

Music and Dance

MUSIC AND DANCE ARE the two universal languages known to the human race. African music and dance are peoples' arts and therefore are an integral part of a community's culture. They are important forms of performance and expression that are found in practically all Mozambican communities. Each community has a song and/or dance that express human involvement in activities ranging from planting and harvesting to initiation and funerals. Every person can sing and dance, and through the two they can as well communicate the message of joy and satisfaction or sorrow and disappointment. People sing when they walk, work, relax, mourn, or pray. While the type of song varies with the occasion, song as part of daily life cuts across the ethnic, gender, and generation divide.

Music and dance share certain commonalities; both encompass many forms and styles. Music encompasses singing, clapping, and drumming. All these activities are usually accompanied by the use of various instruments. Furthermore, Mozambican music, as indeed all African music, tends to be collective and communal. Unless specifically proscribed, it is the norm for dancers to leap into action as the music and/or drums begin to throb. Music is an integral part of dance. Despite the diversity existent in Mozambique because of its many ethnic groups, songs and dances as performances can be categorized based on region, genres, and styles that usually cut across the ethnic divide.

This chapter is divided into five sections. The function of music and dance in Mozambican societies is discussed in the first section. The nature and use of instrumentation is addressed in the next section. Music genre and dance genres are discussed in the third and fourth sections respectively. The chapter concludes by delving into contemporary influences on Mozambican music and dance.

ROLE OF MUSIC AND DANCE IN SOCIETY

Musical games are an integral part of training children in Mozambican communities. Children appreciate music from an early age because they are usually soothed and lulled to sleep with it by their nannies. Lullabies sensitize kids to the significance of music from an early age. The message conveyed is of peace, love, and appreciation, and the subtle message that crying unnecessarily is bad. As the children grow, music becomes a daily routine, which they encounter as stories are narrated about daily activities such as fishing, herding, hunting, and harvesting. Children accompany their older siblings as well as parents to many social gatherings where music is played and people dance. Children soon learn to imitate the songs and dances as they come of age and begin to interact with their playmates. If the music is accompanied with some form of art/instrument, children usually play out the drama of making similar art and imitating its use in their music and dance.

Music and dance are equally significant as means of engaging attention and involving children in learning activities in their early years in elementary school. Coupled with story telling, the performances facilitate the acquisition of knowledge by making learning a pleasurable process for the young learners. Besides, the music and dance constitute an important aspect of the performance arts curriculum.

Mozambican songs and dances are very dynamic as forms of entertainment. They are characterized by stops and starts as well as unexpected accents that give way to smooth lyrical steps. Movement and rhythm are indistinguishable. The harmony between movement and rhythm is apparent in most of the songs and dances. In the traditional society such entertainment was the norm during festive celebrations such as weddings when the couple as well as the guests were entertained. However, Christian chorals are very popular among the faithful, especially in Christian weddings.

During school games, such as soccer or netball, and track events, songs and dances are used to cheer up the players. Some of the songs are specific to a player or players who are known to be good performers. On certain occasions, songs targeting the star(s) of the opposing teams are sung to demoralize them and for the team being supported to capitalize on the other team's low morale or confusion to win. Thus the song is used to influence the outcome of a game by either boosting morale or demoralizing a team or a star player. One of the important aspects of these young composers is their creativity in composing a song and substituting characters to reflect the state of the game. The soloist, who is usually the composer, leads the way, and the rest of the group joins in.

Music and dance are an important part of most rituals pertaining to life events, births, initiations, marriage ceremonies, and funerals. The *Nyau* dancers from the Nyanja community constitute a secretive cult for men who dance at initiation rites. In this case, performance serves an important function that speaks to the coming of age into adulthood, illustrating the joy and triumph that characterizes the initiation ceremony as well as the attendant responsibilities.

Similarly, the Makonde have elaborate homecoming receptions for the newly graduated male initiates. The *Lipiku* dance is an excellent example of art, music, and dance woven together to capture the spirit of victory that is evident among the initiates. Dancers and drummers honor the initiates as they sing in praise of God and seek his strength and power so that the initiates may enjoy life. The girls too are entertained by the special *mdimu* dance after their initiation.

Music and dance reinforce religious beliefs and transcend ordinary entertainment. Healers and diviners use music and dance performances to further their treatments of the sick. The veneration of ancestors as well as prayers and offerings to God are invariably accompanied by some music or ritual dances. In communicating with the other world, diviners are not oblivious to the significance of music and dance in engaging the attention of their clients to the mysteries of the ancestors and God. The Chewa music is also used to entertain and educate the youth about the *myumba ya Chewa,* the Chewa way of life.

Mozambique underwent colonial rule with all its attendant repressive measures and humiliation. Mozambicans resorted to various ways to voice their resentment against colonial oppression. Besides militant uprisings, strikes, and go-slows in workplaces, music became an effective instrument to mobilize the masses to fight against Portuguese colonialism. It is against this setting that *Marrabenta* music gained prominence during the colonial period as a protest against the ills of Portuguese colonialism. The music developed in urban areas and is a fusion of imported European music in African dialects played on improvised materials—homemade guitars, tin cans, and pieces of wood.

Music and dance are critical ingredients of Mozambican culture. Yet during the colonial period, the missionaries frowned on indigenous African music and dance because they saw such ethnic performances as bereft of morality. They discouraged African music and dance on the grounds that they were too full of passion and excitement and therefore unacceptable in churches and sponsored institutions. The situation was reversed after the attainment of independence when the Frelimo government restored African music and dance to its rightful place in society by collecting, preserving, and promoting the expressive art forms of the Mozambican people. The government became directly involved in promoting Mozambican music and dance as part of its cultural revival. In 1978, the Ministry of Education and Culture organized a national dance festival. Besides being well attended, the festival resulted in the creation of numerous organizations and festivals whose primary purpose was to promote Mozambican music.

One of these organizations is the National Song and Dance Company of Mozambique (CNCD), Companhia Nacional de canto e Danca de Mozambique. The group, which comprises dancers, musicians, actors, and storytellers, was founded in 1979 as an amateur dance troupe. It turned professional in 1983 and has since not only received generous funding but has also been instrumental in promoting Mozambican songs locally and abroad. The troupe has visited numerous countries in Africa, Europe, South, Central, and North America, and the Middle East. The troupe's authentic song and dance performances have kept Mozambican culture very much alive in contemporary society.

Nimbu Productions is a similar organization that has also endeavored to promote traditional songs and dances. Not as widely traveled as the CNCD, Nimbu Productions stages performances in various towns in the country and also entertains tourists. Furthermore, they put up exhibitions displaying sculpture and other works of art.

After the attainment of independence in 1975, Mozambican bands proceeded to forge new music forms based on local folk styles and the new African popular music coming from the neighboring countries of the Democratic republic of Congo, Zimbabwe, Tanzania, Zambia, and South Africa.

MUSICAL INSTRUMENTS

African music and dance is incomplete without instruments. Instruments commonly used across the ethnic divide include the drum, the *ngoma,* which is the instrument of choice in the music and dances of most Mozambican communities, including the Makua, Chewa, Chopi, and Makonde. The drum is the most representative African instrument. Drums come in various sizes and shapes. Uncured animal skins are the preferred choice for drumheads because they dry hard and taut. Antelope, zebra, or cowhides are most commonly used. The body of the drum is made from hollowed-out wood, or from a dried gourd. Alternatively, paint cans or long and large cylindrical containers can also be used. Some of the drums are small, while others are huge, averaging three feet in height and two feet in diameter. The drum is played with sticks and/or hands.

While drums are generally used in musical and dance performances, it is important to note that some drums are for specific roles, including rituals, healing, war, and ordinary celebrations. Ritual drums are rarely used outside the occasion for which they are primarily designed. When ritual drums are played people recognize the occasion and the general message being conveyed to the community. Similarly, when they are played on a festive occasion, the mood is usually upbeat and people enjoy themselves by dancing to the rhythm. This is often accompanied with some music and dance.

Other instruments include the *mambilira*, a xylophone with wooden keys that is widely used by the Chewa. It is known as *marimba* among the Shona. The Chopi play the *timbila*, which is also a type of xylophone. These instruments are made of special wood and gourds, the latter of which is made hollow and used as a sound box. Xylophone recordings vary from solo performances to xylophone orchestras with myriad combinations. During a concert there is an average of 8 xylophone players among most of the communities, although the number can be as high as 18 among the Chopi.[1]

Rattles and shakers are equally important. Some are made of tin cans or gourds, which are hollowed out and then filled with pebbles or hard seeds. The tins and gourds are often decorated with many colors. A good example is the marimba among the Chopi.[2] The artist rattles the gourd or tin to produce a rhythmic sound. Marimbas usually accompany the Chopi music and chants. Leg rattles are tied around the dancers' ankles or knees. The dancer uses the rattles as he takes steps that provide rhythmic accompaniment to the musical dance. However, rattles and shakers can also be held in the hand and shaken to produce the desired sound.

Tambourines or frame drums also belong to the foregoing group of rattles and shakers. Tambourines are locally made from improvised materials, which include *sistrum*, a metal and wire shaker, and recycled bottle caps. Tambourines are widely used in traditional dances and as an aid to prayer and worship when used by church choirs in the course of service.

Flutes and whistles are also widely used by Mozambicans. Blowing air against a sharp edge or over a hole in flute or whistle produces sound. In playing the flute, the player changes the note by covering and uncovering the holes. The most common flutes used in Mozambique are made from a dried *matamba* fruit. They are decorated and carved with various shapes.

The foregoing instruments constitute only a fraction of the various instruments that are used by Mozambican communities. Some of the instruments can be played simultaneously in the course of a concert depending on the type of song or dance being performed. Furthermore, improvisation is the norm among children or upstarts who want to imitate the actual performances.

DANCE

Mozambican dances have a regional bent that speaks to the diversity existent in the country. The dances are also closely tied to various factors that have influenced the evolution and development of various cultures within each region. The northern coast of Mozambique has had enormous influences from the Arabs as well as the Portuguese in the course of several centuries. Their religious and cultural influences are evident in the women's celebratory dance called *tufu* or *nsoppe* that is popular in the northern coast of Mozambique. The accompanying songs are of love and happiness and also of humor meant to cheer people up.

Forces from within the country as well as from South Africa have influenced the southern part of Mozambique. Indeed, most of the communities in the southern part of the country have ethnic and cultural ties with their kinsmen in South Africa. The dance exhibits a sense of militancy because it was traditionally performed to prepare warriors for battle or celebrate a military victory. The Nguni warriors introduced the dance into the region from Zululand in South Africa during the Mfecane wars of the nineteenth century. In performing the dance, the troupe dress as if for battle; they brandish their weapons while their steps and movements represent the various stages of war, reconnaissance, pursuit, engagement and actual combat, and victory. The drums reinforce the building tempo. The chanting of war songs adds to the intensity of the dance.

Similarly, the *N'Ganda* dance, which is popular among the communities who live in Niassa province, has a military connotation and was introduced to Mozambique's Niassa province after World War I. The returning veterans who fought for the British against the Germans displayed their military prowess on their return. The prowess parades were internalized and became part of regular activities during celebratory events such as harvest festivals. These themes of military and dance are closely intertwined in contemporary Mozambican music and dance history. Today martial songs and dances that depict the war of liberation as well as the subsequent civil war that engulfed the nation have been embraced by most communities in the country. The performers of these songs and dances brandish wooden weapons—replicas of actual ones—as they step and march in a style reminiscent of what was observed and lived during the tumultuous times.

The *Makwaya* dance, which is performed at weddings, got its roots in the Manica and Sofola provinces. The troupe divides itself into two groups, with one representing the grooms' and the other the brides' families. The scene of canvassing and the subsequent compromise and acceptance by both families and the joy of the couple are best captured by the song and dance, both of which ensure a happy celebration for all the participants. Almost similar in content is the *Semba* dance from Sofala province, a joyful upbeat dance that expresses the deep and emotional feelings of young people in love. It is now widely performed throughout the country.

From the Zambezi province comes the *Niquetxe* dance, which owes its origins to the forced labor that characterized Portuguese colonial rule. The conditions under which Mozambicans were forced to work during colonial rule shortened their lives. Arbitrary and harsh punishments ranging from flogging to hard labor in the hands of monopolies that controlled most of the sectors of the colonial economy gave rise to both overt and latent protests. Niquetxe dance was a performance in memory of the victims of the oppressive colonial system. It was usually performed on the occasion of a death. However, today it is performed at any time of the year.

The *Mapiko* dance among the Makonde is exclusively a men's affair.[3] The dance derives its name from the mask that is worn by the dancers. The mask is carved out of wood and painted in secret. Mapiko is a ritual dance that is performed during special occasions such as initiation or exorcising demons. The accompanying instruments are drums—*ngoma*—and *lupembe,* which is a wind instrument made from animal horns or from wood. The performance attracts many villagers and lasts for several hours.

An important factor that characterizes performers is their lavish use of body art and decoration. The body is decorated in many and varied colors. The lead performers or soloists decorate themselves in a way that makes the occasion special, befitting its intended purpose. The use of masks is common in cases where the identity of the performers and/or soloists is to remain secret or mimic a person or event. In such situations the masks veil the individuals and enable them to take on a new character. The masks allow the performers to exhibit seriousness, beauty, intrigue, or fun depending on the occasion being celebrated.

MUSIC

Timbila

Timbila is a characteristic instrument and music of the Chopi ethnic group, who live in the south coast, north of the capital city of Maputo. Timbila is a wooden xylophone from which has developed a whole genre of music and style associated with the instrument. It is deeply rooted in the Chopi musical tradition and has retained its unique style, which predates the coming of the Portuguese in the late fifteenth century. Children are introduced to Timbila music as early as the age of five or six. Believed to be the most sophisticated method of composition in Mozambique, Timbila orchestras consist of 10 xylophones of 4 sizes. The leader of the orchestra serves as the poet, composer, conductor, and performer. Timbila music is a sensation with its wood-toned sounds and fresh styles of music expressed by the Chopi's tonal language as well as meaningful lyrics.[4]

Eduardo Durao and Venancio Mbande are the two most famous Timbila performers, and their albums have been well received. Another famous Timbila musician is Vanancio, whose band Timbila Ta Venasi graced the signing of the 1992 Peace Accord in Rome that marked the end of the Mozambican civil war. His band has performed in the United States as well in as other parts of Europe. Other famed Timbila performers include Simao, Lourindo, and Tania, who founded the Silitia band and recorded their first album in Paris in 2000. Timbila music is instructive of the persistence of the indigenous musical tradition in contemporary society. The Timbila festival, which is held annually in August in Chopiland, attracts thousands of people, both from within and outside of the locality.[5]

Marrabenta

Marrabenta music is very popular across the ethnic divide in Mozambique.[6] It is the most popular style of modern music in the country. The music is urban in origin and is a hybrid of imported Portuguese music and local languages played on improvised materials. The instruments initially used were guitars fashioned out of tin cans and pieces of wood. Marrabenta music irritated the Portuguese because it partly developed as a protest song and dance through which Mozambicans expressed their resentment against the injustices of the colonial system. It gave them hope as they aspired for freedom in the wake of adversarial relations with their colonial masters. Marrabenta also involved lyrics of social criticism and love.

After the country had attained independence, civil war erupted. In addition, natural disasters such as floods have continued to plague Mozambique. Marrabenta underwent major innovation to cope with the challenges that the country confronted. From the late 1970s music production companies were instrumental in recording artists as well as sponsoring large concerts. The result was the release of several Marrabenta albums, including the compilation *Amanhecer*.

The group Orchestra Marrabenta Star de Mocambique was formed in 1979 under the leadership of long-time performer Wazimbo. The group produced a massive hit with their album Nwahulwana. The Orchestra Marrabenta Star de Mocambique has nurtured several famed Mozambican musicians, including Stewart Sukuma, Chico Antonio, and Jose Mucavel.

CONTEMPORARY INFLUENCES

Besides the more traditionally oriented music and dance and the accompanying instruments outlined above, Mozambicans have embraced more music and dance from outside of the country. The types of influences can generally be grouped into two categories: religious and secular music. Christian hymns are the norm during prayer service. However, the followers of various Christian denominations sing songs in vernacular. In addition, some traditional instruments are now acceptable for use in churches. The clapping of hands, body movement, and African tunes and rhythms are no longer frowned upon. These now constitute an integral part of hymn presentation prayer service. In addition, the myriad instruments discussed above, ranging from drums to tambourines, are used in songs in church. While the Second Vatican Council was definitely the decisive factor in the case of the Roman Catholic Church, the rise of revival/independent churches has equally been instrumental in moderating the conservatism that restricted the language in which the mass had to be said as well as the singing of Christian hymns. Indeed, some African revival churches have embraced cultural practices such as chasing away evil spirits. In the process, African chants, songs, dances, and improvised instruments have been incorporated and form part of the church practice. Traditional musical instruments, music, and dance have enriched Christianity in Mozambican settings by making most converts feel at home in church.

As already noted in chapter one, the ethnic communities in Mozambique are related to their kinsmen in the neighboring countries of Botswana, Malawi, Tanzania, Zambia, Zimbabwe, and South Africa. This is because of the regional interaction and migration that have occurred in central and southern Africa in the last two centuries. Music and dances tend to have a regional bent, with adjacent regions having much in common as result of cross-cultural influences. Furthermore, the boundaries are arbitrary and cut across ethnic groups, placing some members of an ethnic group in one country and others in another. The result has been the development of music and dance whose frontiers extend well beyond the boundaries of Mozambique.

Modern technology and the power of the media have been equally instrumental in the development of music such as rap and reggae, both of which appeal to the youth. This has led to the emergence of not only local rap, but also attempts to have hybrid music that can appeal to a wide array of audiences, both old and young. It is against this backdrop that Marrabenta music has continued to show its hybrid flavor by embracing and incorporating rap. Musicians of both young and older generations best exemplify this endeavor. Lisboa Matavel and Dilon Djindji, both seasoned men of the Marrabenta music, joined forces with young stars, including Chiquito of the Mozambican hip-hop group Mad Level, to produce a sensational album, *Karimbo,* which was produced against the backdrop of the Mozambican floods of 2000. This album brings alive the hypnotic guitar patterns of Marrabenta as well as the rapping of Chiquito, with its contemporary edge. The album was a testament to the inspirational value of music during times of stress. Mozambicans are therefore able to listen to a variety of music genres when they go to live concerts. Jukeboxes as well as radio stations are other media through which Mozambicans listen to music.

Drama and music are part of the curriculum in schools. This has enabled students, especially in rural areas, to keep alive their rich cultural traditions through various performances ranging from songs and dances at sporting events to competitions during drama and music festivals. The use of costumes, traditional instruments, and creativity in composing songs and dances is a testimony to the fact that traditional music and dance are deliberately being nurtured and imparted to the succeeding generation. In this process, cross-cultural influences are the norm rather than the exception. Students from various ethnic groups are sensitized to the rich cultural diversity existent in the country. Thus, cross-cultural influences will continue to define the content and future of Mozambican music and dance.

NOTES

1. Kirsten Walles, "Mozambique," in Toyin Falola, ed., *Teen Life in Africa* (Westport, CT: Greenwood Press, 2004), 167.

2. R. S. James, *Places and Peoples of the World: Mozambique* (New York and Philadelphia: Chelsea House Publishers, 1988), 71.

3. John Stoner, *Makonde* (New York: Rosen Publishing Group, 1998), 30.

4. Hugh Tracey, *Chopi Musicians: Their Music, Poetry, and Instruments* (London and Oxford, UK: International African Institute and Oxford University Press, 1970).

5. Kirsten Walles, "Mozambique," 167.

6. Celso Paco, "A Luta Continua," in Simon Broughton et al., eds., *World Music Volume 1: Africa and the Middle East* (New York: Rough Guides Ltd, Penguin Books, 2000), 579–584.

Glossary

Arbaini.   The end of the Islamic 40-day mourning period.

Assimilado.   Indigenous Africans who were co-opted into the Portuguese colonial system by being given civil rights.

Bacalhao.   Dried salted fish mixed with vegetables.

Buku.   Book.

Canico.   Local reed used in the construction of a house.

Chitala.   House among the Makonde.

Cipitu.   Initiation of girls among the Makonde.

Dashiki.   Western-style T-shirt.

Eid-el-Fitr.   The end of the month of Ramadan.

Eid-el-Kabir.   The end of the hajj.

Eid-el-Maulud.   The birthday of the Prophet Muhammad.

Ichiyao.   Communal work.

Indigenas.   Indigenous Africans who were not classified as assimilados.

Jando.   The Makonde boys' initiation ceremony.

Kilemba.   A kind of bride wealth, *mahari,* given to the father of the bride.

Kuosha maiti.   Islamic ritual of washing of the dead.

Likumbi.   A Makonde house where the initiates are sheltered.

Lipiku.   Makonde dance performed during male initiation ceremony.

Lobola.   Bride wealth paid to the family of the bride by the bridegroom.

Lupembe.   A wind musical instrument.

Macaza.   Shellfish skewed on bamboo twigs and grilled over open fire.

Mahari.   Islamic bride wealth.

Makwaya.   Traditional dance performed at weddings.

Mambilira.   A Chewa xylophone with wooden keys.

Mamwene.   Makua clan elders.

Mapiko.   A dance among Makonde men where performers wear masks.

Marimba.   A Shona musical instrument.

Marrabenta.   Anticolonial music that gained currency during Portuguese colonialism.

Matamba.   A fruit used in making a flute.

Matanga.   Islamic funeral.

Matata.   Clams cooked in wine with finely chopped peanuts and tender young greens or fruits.

Matengusi.   Initiation of girls among the Makua.

Maziko.   Islamic ritual of burial.

Mdimu.   Special dance performed to entertain girls at initiation.

Mkukomela.   An elder who presides over the Makonde initiation ceremony.

Mnobo.   Guardian and mentor of the initiate among the Makonde.

Mudimu.   Initiation ceremonial dance among the Makonde.

Muluku.   God among the Makua.

Mulungu.   God among the Yao.

Mweleko (or Mkaja).   A kind of Islamic bride wealth, *mahari*, given to the mother of the bride.

Mwene.   A Makua elder; also means king of the Mutapa.

Myumba ya Chewa.   The Chewa way of life.

N'Ganda.   Popular dance in Niassa province.

Namku.   Mentor and guardian of the initiate among the Makua.

Ndona.   Lip plug.

Ngoma.   Drum.

Nihuku nowshinga.   Makua ceremony performed on the third day after the burial of the deceased.

Niquetxe.   Popular protest dance dating back to the colonial period.

Nsima.   A type of softer porridge made from corn flour.

Nsoppe.   Women's celebratory dance in the northern coast of Mozambique.

Nyau.   A dance group from the Nyanja who perform at initiation rites.

Piri-piri.   A hot African chili.

Prazero.   A powerful landlord who owned huge land estates and commanded private armies in Mozambique between the seventeenth and nineteenth centuries.

Prazo.   The estate of a prazero.

Ramadan.   30-day fasting period among Muslims.

Sadaq.   Almsgiving.

Sadza.   Traditional corn meal made from corn flour.

Semba. Joyful upbeat dance popular in Sofala province.

Shema. Palm wine.

Sistrum. A metal and wire shaker and recycled bottle caps.

Timbila. A Chopi musical instrument.

Tufu. Women's celebratory dance in the northern coast of the Mozambique.

Utashi (or Kosa). Islamic wedding gift to bride's parents from the groom's family.

Utheka. Local brew.

Bibliography

Abrahams, Roger D. *African Folktales* (New York: Pantheon Books, 1983).

Achebe, Chinua and C. L. Innes, eds. *The Heinemann Book of Contemporary African Short Stories* (Portsmouth, NH: Heinemann, 1992).

Adekunle, Julius O. "East African States." In Toyin Falola, ed., *Africa Volume 1: African History Before 1885* (Durham, NC: Carolina Academic Press, 2000).

Ahanotu, Austin M. "Social Institutions: Kinship Systems." In Toyin Falola, ed., *Africa Volume 2: African Cultures and Societies before 1885* (Durham, NC: Carolina Academic Press, 2000).

Alpers, Edward A. "East Central Africa." In Nehemia Levtzion and Randall L. Pouwels, eds., *The History of Islam in Africa* (Athens: Ohio University Press, 2000).

Alpers, Edward A. *Ivory and Slaves in East Central Africa: Changing Patterns in International Trade to the Later Nineteenth Century* (London: Heinemann, 1975).

Azevedo, Mario Joaquim. *Tragedy and Triumph: Mozambique Refugees in South Africa, 1997-2001* (Portsmouth, NH: Heinemann, 2002).

Bangert, William V., S. J. *A History of the Society of Jesus* (St. Louis, MO: Institute of Jesuit Sources, 1986).

Banham, Martin, Errol Hill, and George Woodyard, eds. *The Cambridge Guide to African and Caribbean Theatre* (Cambridge: Cambridge University Press, 1994).

Bebey, Francis. *African Music: A People's Art,* Josephine Bennett, trans. (New York: Lawrence and Hill, 1976).

Bediako, Kwame. *Christianity in Africa: The Renewal of a Non-Western Religion* (Edinburgh, UK: Edinburgh University Press, 1995).

Bilby, Kenneth. "Music in Africa and the Caribbean." In Mario Joaquim Azevedo, ed., *Africana Studies: A Survey of Africa and the African Diaspora* (Durham, NC: Carolina Academic Press, 1993).

Bowen, Merle L. *The State against the Peasantry: Rural Strategies in Colonial and Postcolonial Mozambique* (Charlottesville: University of Virginia Press, 2000).

Braganti, Nancy and Elizabeth Devine. *Travelers Guide to African Customs and Manners* (New York: St. Martin's Griffin, 1995).

Bravmann, Rene A. *African Islam* (Washington, DC: the Smithsonian Institution Press, 1983).

Bruner, Charlotte H., ed. *The Heinemann Book of African Women's Writing* (Portsmouth, NH: Heinemann, 1993).

Chabal, Patrick. *The Postcolonial Literature of Lusophone Africa* (Evanston, IL: Northwestern University Press, 1996).

Chanda, Jacqueline. *African Arts and Cultures* (Worchester, MA: Davis Publications, 1993).

Chinweizu, Jemie Onwuchekwa. *Decolonizing the African Mind* (Lagos, Nigeria: Pero Press, 1987).

Chinweizu, Jemie Onwuchekwa, ed. *Voices from Twentieth-Century Africa: Griots and Towncriers* (London and Boston: Faber and Faber, 1988).

Christe, Frances and Joseph Hanlon. *African Issues: Mozambique and the Great Flood of 2000* (London, UK: James Currey, 2001).

Coutu, Mia. *Under the Frangipani.* David Brookshaw, trans. (London, UK: Serpents Trail Publishing, 2001).

Couto, Mia. *Voices Made Night.* David Brookshaw, trans. (London, UK: Reed Educational and Professional Publishing, 1990).

Couto, Mia. "The Birds of God." In Chinua Achebe and C. L. Innes, eds., *The Heinemann Book of Contemporary Women's Writing* (Portsmouth, NH: Heinemann, 1992).

Craveirinha, Jose. "The Seed Is in Me." In Gerald Moore and Ulli Beier, eds., *The Penguin Book of Modern African Poetry* (London and New York: Penguin Books, 1998).

Curtin, Philip et al. *African History: From Earliest Times to Independence* (London and New York: Longman, 1995).

De Sousa, Noemia. "Appeal" and "If You Want to Know Me." In Gerald Moore and Ulli Beier, eds., *The Penguin Book of Modern African Poetry* (London and New York: Penguin Books, 1998).

Doney, Meryl. *Musical Instruments* (Milwaukee, WI: Garen Stevens Publishing, 2004).

Elder, Arlene A. "Who Can Take the Multitude and Lock the Cage?: Noemia de Sousa, Micere Mugo, Ellen Kuzwayo: The African Women's Voices of Resistance." *Matatu: Journal of African Culture and Society* 3, 6 (1989): 77–100.

Falola, Toyin. "Intergroup Relations." In Toyin Falola, ed., *Africa Volume 2: African Cultures and Societies before 1885* (Durham, NC: Carolina Academic Press, 2000).

Finnegan, William. *A Complicated War: The Harrowing of Mozambique* (Berkeley: University of California Press, 1992).

Gilbert, Erik and Jonathan T. Reynolds. *Africa in World History* (Upper Saddle River, NJ: Pearson/Prentice Hall, 2004).

Hall, Margaret and Tom Young. *Confronting Leviathan: Mozambique since Independence* (Athens: Ohio University Press, 1997).

Hastings, Adrian. *The Church in Africa, 1450–1950* (Oxford: Clarendon Press, 1994).

Hobsbawn, Eric J. and Terence Ranger, eds. *The Invention of Tradition* (Cambridge: Cambridge University Press, 1992).

Honwana, Raul. *The Life History of Raul Honawana: An Inside View of Mozambique from Colonialism to Independence, 1905–1975,* Allen F. Isaacman, ed. (Boulder, CO: Lynne Rienner, 1988).

Isaacman, Allen F. *Mozambique: The Africanization of a European Institution, the Zambezi Prazos, 1750–1902* (Madison: University of Wisconsin Press, 1972).

Isaacman, Allen F. and Barbara S. Isaacman. *Slavery and Beyond: The Making of Men and Chikunda Ethnic Identities in the Unstable World of South-Central Africa, 1750–1920* (London: Heinemann, 2004).

James, R. S. *Places and Peoples of the World: Mozambique* (New York and Philadelphia: Chelsea House Publishers, 1988).

Jorge, Lidia. *The Murmuring Coast.* Natalia Costa and Ronald W. Sousa, trans. (Minneapolis and London: University of Minnesota Press, 1995).

Kaplan, Irving et al. *Area Handbook for Mozambique,* 2nd ed. (Washington, DC: 1977).

Kasfir, Sidney Littlefield. *Contemporary African Art* (London: Thames and Hudson, 1999).

Kayongo-Male, Diane and Philista Onyango. *The Sociology of the African Family* (London and New York: Longman, 1984).

Khapoya, Vincent B. *The African Experience: An Introduction* (Englewood Cliffs, NJ: Prentice-Hall, 1994).

Kubat, Kazimierz and Edwin Mpokasaye. "Excerpts of Makua Traditions," http://www.sds-ch.ch/centre/artyk/article/makua.htm. Cited February 26, 2006.

Laure, Jason and Ettagale Blauer. *Enchantment of the World: Mozambique* (Chicago: Childrens Press, 1995).

Magaia, Lina. *Dumba Nengue: Run for Your Life—Peasant Tales of Tragedy in Mozambique* (Trenton, NJ: Africa World Press, 1988).

Magaia, Lina. "Madalena Returned from Captivity." In Charlotte H. Bruner, ed., *The Heinemann Book of African Women's Writing* (Portsmouth, NH: Heinemann, 1993).

Malangatana,Valente. "To the Anxious Mother." In Okpewho, Isidore, ed., *The Heritage of African Poetry* (Essex, UK: Longman Group, 1985).

Mankell, Henning. *Secrets in the Fire.* Anne Connie Stuksrud, trans. (Toronto: Annick Press, 2003).

Mbiti, John S. *Concepts of God in Africa* (New York/Washington: Praeger Publishers, 1970).

Mbiti, John S. *Love and Marriage in Africa* (London: Longman Group Limited, 1973).

Mbiti, John S. *Prayers in African Religion* (Maryknoll, NY: Orbis Books, 1975).

Middleton, Nick. *Kalashnikovs and Zombie Cucumbers* (London, UK: Sinclair-Stevenson, 1994).

Mohl, Max. *Masterpieces of the Makonde* (Heidelberg: Max Mohl, 1989).

Montgomery, Bertha and Constance Nabwire. *Cooking the African Way* (New York: Lerner Publishing, 1988).

Moore Gerald and Ulli Beier, eds. *The Penguin Book of Modern African Poetry* (New York and London: Penguin Books, 1998).

Mudenge, S. I. *A Political History of Munhumutapa* (Harare, Zimbabwe: Zimbabwe Publishing House, 1986).

Munslow, Barry. "Maputo." In Kevin Shillington, ed., *The Encyclopedia of African History, Volume II* (New York and London: Fitzroy Dearborn, 2005).

Munslow, Barry. "Mozambique after Machel." *Third World Quarterly* 10, 1 (1988).

New, W. H. "Colonial Literatures." In Bruce King, ed., *New National and Postcolonial Literatures: An Introduction* (Oxford, UK: Clarendon Press, 1996).

Newitt, Malyn. *A History of Mozambique* (Bloomington and Indianapolis: Indiana University Press, 1995).

Okpewho, Isidore, ed. *The Heritage of African Literature* (Essex, UK: Longman Group, 1985).

Olupona, Jacob K. and Sulayman S. Nyang, eds. *Religious Plurality in Africa: Essays in Honour of John S. Mbiti* (Berlin and New York: Mouton de Gruyter, 1993).

Paco, Celso. "A Luta Continua." In Simon Broughton et al., eds., *World Music Volume 1: Africa and the Middle East* (New York: Rough Guides/Penguin Books, 2000).

Ramsay, F. James. *Global Studies: Africa* (Guildford, CT: Dushkin/McGraw-Hill, 1999).

Sandler, Bea et al. *The African Cookbook* (New York: Carol Publishing Group, 1993).

Saul, John S. *Recolonization and Resistance: Southern Africa in the 1990s* (Trenton, NJ: Africa World Press, 1993).

Scheub, Harold. *The African Storyteller: Stories from African Oral Traditions* (Dubuque, IA: Kendall/Hunt Publishing Company, 1990).

Scheub, Harold. *A Dictionary of African Mythology: The Mythmaker as Storyteller* (Oxford, UK: Oxford University Press, 2000).

Schneider, Harold K. *The Africans: An Ethnological Account* (Upper Saddle River, NJ: Prentice-Hall, 1981).

Stoner, John. *Makonde* (New York: Rosen Publishing Group, 1998).

Sundkler, Benght and Christopher Steed. *A History of the Christian Church in Africa* (Cambridge: Cambridge University Press, 2000).

Tracey, Hugh. *Chopi Musicians: Their Music, Poetry, and Instruments* (London and Oxford, UK: International African Institute and Oxford University Press, 1970).

Trimingham, J. Spencer. *Islam in East Africa* (Oxford, UK: Clarendon Press, 1964).

Trimingham, J. Spencer. *The Influence of Islam upon Africa* (London and New York: Longman, 1980).

United Nations Educational, Social, and Cultural Organization. "Education for All: Report of Mozambique." http://www2.unesco.org/wet/countryreports/mozambique/contents.html (2003).

United States Agency for International Development. "Mozambique." http://www.usaid.gov/locations/sub-saharan_africa/countries/mozambique/index.html.

United States of America. "CIA World Factbook: Mozambique." https://www.cia.gov/cia/publications/factbook/geos/mz.html (2005).

Urdang, Stephanie. *And Still They Dance: Women, War, and the Struggle for Change in Mozambique* (New York: Monthly Review Press, 1989).

Vansina, Jan. *Oral Tradition as History* (Madison: University of Wisconsin Press, 1985).

Vera, Yvonne ed. *Opening Spaces* (Portsmouth, NH: Heinemann, 2000).

Walles, Kristen. "Mozambique." In Toyin Falola, ed., *Teen Life in Africa* (Westport, CT: Greenwood Press, 2004).

Willet, Frank. *African Art and Early History* (London, UK: Thames and Hudson, 1978).

Wright, John. "Mfecane." In Kevin Shillington, ed., *Encyclopedia of African History* (New York/London: Fitzroy Dearborn Publishers, 2005).

Index

About the Author

GEORGE O. NDEGE is Associate Professor of History at St. Louis University.

Recent Titles in
Culture and Customs of Africa

Culture and Customs of Ghana
Steven J. Salm and Toyin Falola

Culture and Customs of Egypt
Molefi Kete Asante

Culture and Customs of Zimbabwe
Oyekan Owomoyela

Culture and Customs of Kenya
Neal Sobania

Culture and Customs of South Africa
Funso Afolayan

Culture and Customs of Cameroon
John Mukum Mbaku

Culture and Customs of Morocco
Raphael Chijioke Njoku

Culture and Customs of Botswana
James Denbow and Phenyo C. Thebe

Culture and Customs of Liberia
Ayodeji Oladimeji Olukoju

Culture and Customs of Uganda
Kefa M. Otiso

Culture and Customs of the Central African Republic
Jacqueline Woodfork

Culture and Customs of Zambia
Scott D. Taylor

Culture and Customs of Angola
Adebayo Oyebade